MW00642172

TRAUMA

AN OPEN DOOR

PAUL FERNANDEZ

WITH ADDITIONAL COMMENTARY BY
FRANK HAMMOND AND BILL BANKS

TRAUMA:
AN OPEN DOOR

by Paul Fernandez
with Additional Commentary by Frank Hammond and Bill Banks

ISBN 10: 0892284544
ISBN 13: 9780892284542

Edited by the Staff at Impact Christian Books

DISTRIBUTED BY:

IMPACT CHRISTIAN BOOKS, INC.

332 Leffingwell Ave., Suite 101
Kirkwood, MO 63122

WWW.IMPACTCHRISTIANBOOKS.COM

TABLE OF CONTENTS

DEDICATION

To my loving and faithful wife Eve, whose contribution is immeasurable. Everything I have written is just as much her experience as it is mine. Her many hours of prayer, discernment, study and participation in the deliverance ministry made victory possible. We are full and equal partners in the Lord's work.

For a full list of Impact's titles, refer to the website above or use your camera with the **QR Code**

INTRODUCTION

- The social anxiety and rejection issues of a 57-yr-old are supernaturally traced to *trauma* he experienced when his father punched his mother in the stomach while he was in the womb.

- Torturous voices keeping a young man away from church are shown to stem from when, as an infant, he was thrown *traumatically* towards a wall by his drunken father.

- A mother is shown how her son received a destructive spirit of rage as he was conceived while she was subjected to the *trauma* of rape.

- A young man plagued with a life of drugs, alcohol and acts of indecent exposure discovers that it all began with *traumatic* experiences from sexual exhibitionisms of a babysitter.

These testimonies are from real people; people who came to Paul and Eve Fernandez in search of ministry because of the ache in their hearts and oppression weighing on them. What links their stories together is the negative effect trauma had on their lives, continuing well after the event. In a much more powerful sense, though, what links their stories is that they experienced triumph over the *spirit of trauma* through the bondage-breaking power of Jesus.

That is the message of hope brought to light through this book. Trauma does not have to have the last word. Rather, trauma can be turned into the beginning of a miraculous work of Heaven in our lives. The Holy Spirit has worked miracles of healing and deliverance in the lives of so many, and we are grateful for each one.

No one is immune from the effects of trauma, and there is no shame in seeking counseling; Jesus Himself is called the Wonderful Counselor. Everyone, regardless of social status and upbringing, faces potential damage to their personality through traumatic experiences. Trauma can come through something as common as rejection of a young person at school. Trauma can also come from growing up in a violence-filled, dysfunctional home.

Where there is an absence of love in a home, trauma is often prowling near by. Divorce can have traumatizing effects on the children involved. So, too, the death of a loved one can wound a child deeply, and create an obstacle to their emotional growth and maturity.

Others types of trauma are forced through real-life cruelty. We have ministered to survivors of sexual abuse including rape, and their testimonies are included. Many in the world around us on any given day may be victims of abuse, but we do not know because their scars are on the inside.

Trauma can also come through fear. Witnessing a death or being in a serious car accident can result in trauma to our soul. Soldiers come back from war with various degrees of trauma.

Really, no one is immune from an encounter with trauma, and no one is immune from the attack of the enemy that often follows traumatic experiences.

THE BIBLE AS A RECORD

The Bible is an amazing book, in part because it is a record of people who faced extreme traumatic circumstances and pressures. God gave us this record of their lives so that we can draw encouragement and strength from their triumphs over trauma.

Joseph, for instance, faced trauma when he was rejected by his brothers and sold into slavery in a foreign land. He again faced trauma when falsely accused and sent to prison. The triumph he experienced over his traumatic circumstances came because of the favor of God. His life turned to blessing, with him being named second in command of all the land of Egypt, the leading nation of his day. When he emerged from these trials, he was able to state through the names of his sons, *"God has made me forget all my toil and all my father's house,"* and *"God has caused me to be fruitful in the land of my affliction."*

Daniel faced trauma when falsely accused of disrespecting the King, simply by kneeling and worshipping his God. He faced traumatic pressure, again, when the sentence handed down was death by hungry lions. Daniel emerged triumphant and, like Joseph, became second in command to a pagan world superpower, Babylon.

Scriptures teaches us how trauma played a role in the lives of David, Saul, Mary and Joseph, Peter, Paul and so many others in the Bible.

Why did God take so much care to record their stories and to relate their traumatic situations?

Because God wants to keep hope alive in our hearts when we face traumatic situations. Their trials and tribulations were meant *for our benefit.*

God sent His Son on a rescue mission for mankind, and this required facing the trauma of rejection, slander, accusation, trial, scourging and eventually a criminal's death on a cross. When Jesus triumphed over the trauma of it all, the wall (veil) between us and God *tore in half!* A doorway to the throne of Heaven was opened and this door stands open for us to this day.

It is because of trauma and pressure that we remember the Bible so well. In fact, the triumph over trauma is what sets the Bible apart. This is not by chance. God wants to get this message across to us today, and to any who are trapped in a world of fear, tied in the chains and shackles of trauma.

HEAVEN IS COMING TO EARTH

God's will and heart is set against trauma. This is confirmed for us in the Lord's Prayer. This unique prayer is a statement of intent. God intends to bring the way things are in Heaven down to us on Earth: *"Thy will be done on Earth as it is in Heaven."*

In Heaven, there is no trauma.

When Heaven comes to Earth, it will establish its reign at the end of the age. In the meantime, Heaven comes to Earth when the power of the Holy Spirit breaks the chains of torment and fear associated with trauma, whether in our lives or in the lives of those around us. As the light of Heaven appears, darkness flees. The presence of Heaven on Earth today drives away the dark cloud of Satan's torment and effect.

THE SPIRIT OF TRAUMA

Life is never simple, and healing from trauma can take time. As the saying confirms, God uses the passage of time to heal wounds. But the question before us today is this:

- Have the traumatic situations in our past been properly addressed and has time caused those wounds to heal?

or

- Has the enemy gained a foothold in our life through our past, such that traumatic experiences affect our ability to function today.

Sadly, many people are living damaged lives, boxed in by fear and instability brought on by the *spirit of trauma*. Many are unaware of the delivering and healing power of the Holy Spirit to bring change. They have been conditioned by the lies of the enemy, that their situation is hopeless and set in stone. Despite what the enemy whispers in our ear, nothing is set in stone. God is a problem-solving, solutions-oriented force for good in our lives. There is hope in Jesus.

By exploring breakthroughs against the tormenting *spirit of trauma*, we will identify the source of many behavioral problems, and the root cause of some emotional and mental struggles. We endeavor to deal decisively with the *spirit of trauma*, to overcome its lingering effect, and as this foe is vanquished, to give glory for the triumph to come to Jesus.

1

THE BROKEN MIRROR,
A GARDEN IN DISREPAIR

I have been led by the Lord to view the human personality, what some call the human psyche or soul, as a *beautiful mirror*, a polished, crystal piece designed with great care by the hands of the Master. Each of us come into this world with a pristine mirror inside, a mirror without fingerprints and without blemish.

> I will praise You, for **I am fearfully and wonderfully made**;
> **marvelous are Your works**, and that my soul knows very well.
>
> Ps 139:14

This is how we are created from Heaven's perspective, regardless of what circumstances follow us into this world. This mirror reflects light. The light it reflects is the light of Heaven itself. You can catch a glimpse of this light shining outward through the eyes of a child.

The enemy of our soul, Satan, sees our beauty and knows what we are, by virtue of our Creator. This drives him into rage. He cannot have what we have, for he forfeited his right to Heaven's glory (Isaiah 14). Also, he sees the perfection in us and *fears our potential.*

Psalm 139 says we are "fearfully" made. I see this truth two ways: we are that beautiful mirror placed within each of us meant to reflect the light of Heaven, but because of this light we instill *fear* in the heart of our spiritual enemy.

> **We are "fearfully made," and because of this, we are**
> **"a fearful sight" for the enemy. That light strikes terror**
> **in the mind of the unredeemable foe of Heaven, Satan**
> **himself.**

In his misery, Satan (also known as Lucifer) lives out his few, remaining days as *the god of this present age*. His age is coming to an end, and he knows his time is short. Therefore, he focuses his efforts on devising ways to snuff out the light. He develops schemes to shatter the beautiful mirror of our soul.

Victims of his "weaponized" trauma bear the effect in the form of cracked mirrors (shattered personalities), and are in desperate need of repair. When these victims look in the mirror of their soul, they see distortions of their true selves looking back at them. Some light shines, but it is like the disjointed rays of light coming from a cracked mirror.

Jesus knows us. He came to heal the broken-hearted and, in that sense, restore the prestine mirror of our personality (our soul). He is capable of handling each unique case with the necessary care. He yearns for the chance to restore the beauty for which we were intended, for when He does, He honors His Father, the Creator, by doing so. With a soul restored, we can then reflect the light of Heaven again.

Jesus is also intent on putting fear back in the heart of the enemy. When the enemy sees the light of Heaven reflecting off a soul once again, it is a sign of the overwhelming power of the Kingdom of Heaven over the Kingdom of darkness. We are once again seen to be "fearful," because we have been "fearfully and wonderfully *re-made*."

The cry from Heaven at the moment of restoration onwards becomes:

Touch not mine anointed, and do my prophets no harm!

1 Chron 16:22 KJV

Jesus is the God of *restoration*. He has earned this title through His faithful sacrifice on the Cross, to its full and bitter end. His will to restore us today is vividly demonstrated in an encounter He had with a leper in Matthew 8.

> When He had come down from the mountain, great multitudes
> followed Him. And behold, a leper came and worshiped Him,
> saying, "**Lord, if You are willing, You can make me clean**." Then
> Jesus put out His hand and touched him, saying, "**I am willing;
> be cleansed**." Immediately his leprosy was cleansed.
>
> Matt 8:1–3, NKJV

Jesus was willing, *without hesitation*, to lift the oppression of leprosy from the man. In an equally powerful sense, however, Jesus intended to wipe away the trauma in this life from having lived as a social outcast, a despised and shunned leper.

Imagine, for a moment, the trauma that came into this man's life from being pushed away from human companionship by fear of contagion. Imagine the daily trauma to this man's soul as he saw the look of fear on the faces of those around him, knowing his disfiguration caused that terror in their eyes. Without a doubt, the mirror of this poor man's soul had been shattered. Added to the grief and pain of his disease were the insults of rejection and abandonment by those around him.

Jesus took care of both issues in this man's life – the outward and the inward disfiguration.

The blows of the enemy that come against us to shatter the mirror of our soul are described as "fiery darts" by Paul the Apostle:

> Above all, taking the shield of faith with which you will be able
> to quench all the **fiery darts of the wicked one**.
>
> Eph 6:16

This is a powerful description of the attack of the enemy through trauma. These fiery weapons are meant to shatter the mirror of the soul, but also to burn long after they have hit their mark. God knows what we are up against with trauma, and uses Paul to describe perfectly the flaming arrows of trauma sent against us.

A personality damaged by trauma shows signs of emotional distress; fear rules over this soul with an insecurity around others and a sense of abandonment by both God and man. More severe cases of trauma are evidenced by mental instability and breakdown. The most severe cases show evidence of alternative personalities, in an attempt to hide from further trauma by becoming someone entirely different.

Severe rejection and severe trauma can both contribute to a split in personality, but no problem is too big for a loving God. He is a problem-solving, solutions-oriented Deliverer, who works to unlock the doors and gates of bondage in our lives. Jesus released the power of the *Spirit of the Lord* to work miracles and to the heal the lepers, inside and out.

ANOTHER PICTURE OF THE SOUL:
THE GARDEN OF GOD

There is another image I have been led by the Lord to present to you concerning the soul, and this is a *garden*.

The *personality* consists of three parts of a man or woman: the mind, emotions and human will. These areas of a human personality constitute a garden of sorts in the eyes of our Creator.

When they function together in a healthy way, good fruit is produced in the garden of our soul, and this has an effect on not just us but on the lives of those around us.

Why is this so important to God and so frightening to the devil? Because the good fruit of a righteous soul has an *eternal* effect. We may not know how or in what way, but inviting the presence of the Holy Spirit to make His home within us will leave a lasting imprint on the lives of others around us; we accept this as true because God's Word tells us it is so.

It is therefore no wonder that the enemy seeks to choke the vitality of our garden, and keep us from producing good fruit. He loses when eternal fruit is harvested for the Kingdom of Heaven.

> I have chosen you, and ordained you, that ye should go and bring forth fruit, and **that your fruit should** *remain*: that whatsoever ye shall ask of the Father in my name, he may give it you.
>
> John 15:16 KJV

Gardens that produce good fruit are a delight to God who looks down from Heaven and is pleased. Indeed, *God is gardener.* He placed the first man and woman in a Garden named *Eden,* and we are told He enjoyed walking through it (Gen 3:8).

Likewise, God plants a garden in each of us when we are born; it is part of our makeup as humans to be a source of delight to our Creator, much like Eden. The enemy of man does not want us to know this.

The devil does not want you to know that God sees a beautiful garden within you for His delight.

WEEDS, THORNS AND NETTLES

Our gardens were created to grow beautifully. However, in a world filled with trauma, most gardens quickly take on thorns. Proverbs 24 describes a garden that grows fruit (i.e., a vineyard) but the field of crops is in a state of disrepair. The wall surrounding the garden, the "hedge of protection," is broken down and the land is overgrown with thorns and nettles. This garden more accurately describes the state of the soul of many in today's troubled world.

The garden is overgrown with thorns and nettles. *Thorns* cause pain and restrict movement; they prevent our growth and keep us caged. It is difficult to grow and mature when we are trapped in a cage surrounded by thorns. *Nettles* are a poisonous shrub; they release toxins into our body to drain us of our vitality and strength, they stick us and harass us to keep us angry and disturbed. The purpose of these two types of weeds is to block our progress toward peace, restoration and wholeness and to leave us with a sense of instability in God's love.

The result of thorns and nettles is that we become stuck in a rut of recurring panic, stress and strain – what the world calls *post traumatic stress.*

THE CARE OF THE GARDEN: A PARTNERSHIP

Anyone who has spent time planting a garden knows it requires work. This is true of the garden of our soul. We have been tasked with tending our garden, just as Adam and Eve were tasked with tending the Garden of Eden.

We have the responsibility to address the weeds and thorns that try to take root and choke the eternal fruit from coming from within us. Our efforts to keep the garden functioning righteously pleases Heaven and the One who sits on the Throne in Heaven. He joins us in partnership, so that in farming terms, He "adds to our crop" and "increases our yield." What must we learn to do? Guard our garden.

"GUARD THE GARDEN"

Proverbs 4 speaks of the type of guarding necessary for one's soul to function in a healthy manner and keep producing good fruit:

> Keep [guard] thy heart with all diligence; for out of it are the issues of life.
>
> Prov 4:23 KJV

Our role is to *guard the garden*. When we do what is required in the natural realm, to maintain a healthy protective hedge, the Holy Spirit does the heavy lifting, to strengthen us and to even multiply our efforts. Walking daily with Jesus is much like a partnership focused on gardening, and the fruit produced is friendship, love and respect between you and Heaven itself. Friendship with Heaven? *Now that is worth the effort!*

A CROWN OF THORNS

Jesus had to walk through persecution, rejection and trauma. He knows firsthand the burning, bruising sensation of facing the brunt of what the world has to offer. When faced with the most extreme pressure forced on a human being, He did not allow his soul to be damaged, or to disintegrate from His true self. He remained *stable in all His ways.* That tells us there is hope for all, even if we spend a portion of our life learning how to keep ourself stable in His love, despite the storms raging outside.

To emphasize this point, Jesus wore a crown of thorns. Do you see the significance of this act? He took the curse of the thorns intended for us in our "garden," meaning He took the trauma and affliction of our sins.

Now let this thought sink in: because of the humility and willingness of His sacrifice, He now wears a crown of Kingship ("many kingly crowns," Rev 19:12).

When we walk with Jesus, we share with Him in His victory over the curse of those thorns. We set down our own crown of thorns from the trauma of this life and accept, with overwhelming thankfulness, the crown He gives us. Why would He give us a crown? Because we are the King's kids!

> Finally, there is laid up for me **the crown of righteousness,** which the Lord, the righteous Judge, will give to me on that Day, and not to me only but also **to all who have loved His appearing.**   Paul, 2 Tim 4:8 NKJV

And again in Revelation:

> I will **give you the crown of life**.
>
> Jesus speaking to His followers
> Rev 2:10 NKJV

Praise God! *There is hope in Jesus!*

LIFE AND DEATH ARE BEFORE US

Today, as wracked by trauma as we are, God is offering us life, abundant life. First, we must learn who our enemy is however. Jesus makes clear the source of trauma in John 10:

> The thief does not come except to **steal**, and to **kill**, and to **destroy**. I have come that they may have life, and that they may have it more abundantly.
>
> John 10:10

Trauma tries to steal our peace. Trauma tries to kill our sense of security in God as our Protector. Trauma, if we let it, will try to destroy our relationship with Heaven altogether. This is not the will of God but the will of the enemy of God, the thief who comes to *steal, kill* and *destroy*.

So we have a choice before us today: blessing or curse, life or death. I urge you to set aside the thousands of questions pertaining to *how* God will resolve the trauma in your life, and trust that if you choose life and blessing, He will meet you and lead you out of the pit of despair. He will reward you for this act of courage to look to Him.

> I have placed before you life and death, the blessing and the curse. So choose life in order that you may live, you and your descendants, by loving the Lord your God, by obeying His voice, and by holding close to Him...
>
> Deut 30:15–16, NASB

2

TRAUMA: AN OPEN DOOR
(FOR SATAN)

In order to find our way out of trauma, it is important to understand who our enemy is and what his purposes are. We know that God has not given us the spirit of fear...

> For God **has not** given us a *spirit of fear*, but of power and of love and of a **sound mind**.
> 2 Tim 1:7

Fear and an unsound mind do not come from God; rather, God is the source of *soundness* of mind. His will is to restore soundness to our minds.

Along these lines, His love is a perfect love, and perfect love casts out fear:

> There is no fear in love, but **perfect love drives out fear**, because fear involves punishment
> 1 John 4:18

Fear comes in part out of fear of punishment. Jesus took the punishment for us on the Cross. If we think that the traumatic experiences we have been through are a form of punishment from God, read the verse above and immerse yourself in His unconditional love. Jesus came to "cast out" or to "drive out" fear, including the demonic *spirit of fear.*

In the same manner that Jesus "cast out" unclean spirits, so we read here that His love "casts out" fear. The similarity in casting out (or driving out) fear, and casting out or driving out unclean spirits, is *not by coincidence.* Everyone experiences fear at times in their life. But when we become overwhelmed by fears, we become susceptible to the influence of the *spirit of fear.* This is an alive but invisible creature, an unclean spirit, who seeks to set up his home within us and to rule over us. He desires to steer our decisions and to derail the effectiveness of our life.

Jesus, on the opposite side, came to bring us abundant life:

> I am come that they **might have life**, and that they might **have it more abundantly**.
>
> John 10:10, KJV

An abundant life does not consist of material things. Jesus addresses our need for such things in His "Sermon on the Mount." No, the abundant life spoken of is abundant because of the overwhelming presence of peace and stability. It is an inner abundance; an inner strength.

> Peace I leave you, My peace I give you; not as the world gives, do I give to you. Do not let your hearts be troubled, nor fearful.
>
> Jesus Speaking, John 14:27 NASB

Scripture is clear that those things that seek to pull us away from peace and stability are contrary to the will of God, and thus evil in nature.

GAINING ENTRY

The goal of an evil spirit is to gain entry to a person's life and to claim ownership of the body as his "house." Jesus explains this when He describes a demon wandering through dry places. As Jesus outlines for us, when a wandering evil spirit approaches a person, it must first determine that person's *condition of receptiveness*. If the condition is right, the demon will try to enter.

A person does not acquire a demon merely by walking down the street. There is a natural hedge in a mature adult, the human will, which resists intrusion by evil spirits. But without this hedge in place, and in certain traumatic environments, evil spirits can try to get a foothold and make that person a host or vessel.

A few conditions come immediately to mind: a door can be

opened through *inheritance* because of the sins of the parents or grandparents; a door can opened by *yielding to sin* on an ongoing basis (showing willful intent); and a door can be opened during moments of *extreme fear*. What is another way to say extreme fear? "Trauma." Let's take brief look at all three doors.

ENTRY BY INHERITANCE

Curses are consequences of walking outside of God's counsel and advice. God knows that leaving His territory and stepping into the devil's territory is going to have consequences, and these can pass from one generation to the next. A curse is powerless without a spirit to enact it; thus, behind every curse is an evil spirit enacting its effect.[1]

Scripture informs us that emotional, mental and even physical problems may be based in the actions of previous generations of our family. Exodus 20:4-5, for instance, lists a curse as punishment for idol worship, and this can last up to the "third or fourth generations" of descendants. When we think of idols today, we think of statues of deities or objects used in occult rituals. However, an idol exists first and foremost *in the heart*. Whatever we exalt from our heart (good or bad) can become an idol. As a follower of Jesus, whatever we place *above* Him in our heart thus serves as an idol. Jesus hinted at this when He said that man "cannot serve two masters." One has to take priority over the other.

Idols are everywhere in today's society. People idolize education and educational degrees. Christians sometimes idolize their church or their pastor. Churches sometimes idolize money as a means to growth.

---

1 Refer to the Appendix for a prayer to renounce and break curses. Edited from *The Breaking of Curses*, by Frank Hammond. More information is available at the back of the book.

There are other sources of inherited trouble than just idolatry. Deuteronomy 23:2 describes a curse that comes upon the bloodline from an illegitimate birth. An evil spirit will seek to enact that curse as long as it can, up to the tenth generation, unless the curse is broken. Jesus is a specialist when it comes to breaking curses because He became a curse for us at the Cross. This is why the sky darkened, the light of Heaven fled, and the Father turned His eyes away, because Jesus took our curses with Him to the grave. He buried them for us, before He emerged from the tomb alive and free, as He is today.

Jesus did not remove curses at the Cross, He released the power for them *to be broken.* It is our task to appropriate the work He accomplished on the Cross, and to bring His curse-breaking power into our life and into the lives of our family.

The curse from an illegitimate birth in Deuteronomy 23 is of note. It speaks to the fact that doors can be opened to evil spirits as early as *conception.* A spirit can attack a child who is still in the womb.

ENTRY BY OVERT SIN

The second door of entry for an unclean spirit is by living in a state of spiritual uncleanliness, known as sin. This prolonged environment of uncleanliness is a welcome mat to spirits who are by nature "unclean."

The pull of temptation is present in everyone's life. Even Paul cried out for help against sin in Romans 7, the same Paul who is responsible for writing more than half the New Testament! So, sin abounds.

There is a line to be crossed, however, when temptation turns into *willful* sin, and willful sin becomes an *addiction.* It is when sin becomes compulsive that a person should consider that he or she may be in a form of spiritual bondage to a unclean spirit.

Jesus reached out to everyday men, fishermen, to find His disciples. He told them that if they followed Him, He would make them "fishers of men." Satan is a thief. He sees the work of Heaven and counterfeits it. Since Jesus is a "fisher of men," Satan also is a "fisher of men." He uses temptation as his bait, over and over again, until either we resist him and he flees, or he snares us in bondage.

Within each of us is a spiritual tug-of-war. Our flesh wants to take the poisoned bait offered by the *god of this present age,* while our spirit wants to take the bait that came as a gift from Heaven, the "bread of life."

> Sin does not automatically result in demonic bondage. The love of sin, however, does.

The goal of an evil spirit is to bring into a man the attributes of the spirit's master, Satan. The master of demons, Satan, comes to steal, kill and destroy. While demons may not have the power to kill the flesh, they have the power to steal, kill and destroy the peace and joy we could experience in the flesh. This is why they are referred to as "tormentors." We are told to stand up for our rights against them, rights given to us by Jesus. We are told to resist:

> Resist the devil, and he will flee from you.   James 4:7

Resistance means pushing back against the enemy; this is necessary in the areas of our life where he seeks to derail us. "To resist" is a key to victory over many things, and when combined with the supernatural power of the Holy Spirit, the agent of Heaven itself, mountains in our lives will move. But today many have not been taught to resist sin.

To make matters worse, we find pressures on modern man that were not present a century ago, like the abundance of flashing screens posting pornographic content with lustful intent. That is just one example.

The goal of living a healthy, Heaven-oriented life is to be a reflection the nature of the Kingdom of Heaven; to be ruled by the Spirit of the Lord instead of a spirit in our flesh. Self control, or "temperance," is one of the good fruits of the Holy Spirit:

> But the fruit of the Spirit is love, joy, peace, longsuffering, kindness, goodness, faithfulness, gentleness, **self-control**. Against such there is no law.
>
> Gal 5:22-23 NKJV

Self-control means stirring up our willpower to resist. Each person is faced with challenges as to how to bring their flesh under the control of the Holy Spirit.

Evil spirits are like insects; insects eat fruit. For the Christian, the most obvious effect of unclean or evil spirits is to eat away the fruit of the Spirit. When a swarm of insects gets done picking over good fruit, the fruit becomes far less appealing.

A life not filled with good fruit may be in need of deliverance from the bondage of tormentors in his or her life. The doorway of recurring sin can thus affect the Christlike witness in a believer's life as evidenced by the fruit of the Spirit.

ENTRY BY TRAUMA

The third door of entry for evil spirits is less obvious. Satan is a predator and his demons function in a predatory manner. It is unfortunately in line with their predatory nature to take advantage of times of trauma to attempt entry into a life.

The Apostle Peter says that Satan prowls about like a *predatory lion*, seeking those whom he may devour:

> Be sober, be vigilant; because your adversary the devil, as a roaring lion, walketh about, seeking **whom he may devour**...
>
> 1 Peter 5:8

Satan devours by trampling on the righteousness, peace and joy in our life. As he prowls, traumatic moments can be the most subtle of doors by which predatory spirits gain entry. The panic, disorientation and rush of emotions associated with a traumatic experience can become the cover for these enemies of light to infiltrate and cast a shadow over a soul, and thus create bondage to fear and the fear of trauma.

The fruit born from the *spirit of trauma* is fear and anxiety. The spirit also brings with it insecurity and especially a lack of a security in Jesus. Often sleep problems (insomnia) arise, as does chronic nervousness, depression and hopelessness, and physical issues from the wear and tear all this has on us. More severe cases bring mental torment to the point of illness.

The goal of a *spirit of trauma* is to guide us into poor life decisions aimed at protecting us from further trauma, in a form of extreme self-preservation. This is similar to how sin patterns work, they tend to lead us in downward spirals where bad decisions lead to bad outcomes, and to more sin. So too with trauma, bad outcomes can lead to bad decisions. Jesus is willing and ready to step in and stop this spiral as we ask Him.

EARLY TRAUMA, EARLY ENTRY

My wife, Eve, and I ministered to thousands in need of deliverance. Over the years of counsel we developed what became a breakthrough question to ask in each ministry session.

When operating in unison with the anointing of God, one simple question has enabled us to discover when the most troubling spirits came into a person's life. This question can do the same for you and for those you minister to as well.

The question that unlocks so many doors is this: *What is your earliest recollection?* The earliest recollection in one's life is almost always related to a traumatic experience.

When the individual seeking deliverance begins to open the door to their heart through honest recollection, words of knowledge and the discerning of Spirits often come from the Lord to magnify the effectiveness of this moment. Sometimes the Lord will even bring to remembrance a moment in early life far beyond the human ability to remember.

Under normal circumstances, there can be a fear of exposure in operation, and a fear of revealing true feelings of the heart. For this reason, *we do not* ask people to describe an early trauma. Instead we ask for their earliest recollections in life. This is far less intimidating for people. Then we rely on the Holy Spirit to spur the memory of the person seeking counsel.

Looking back now on years of ministry, we can say that in one hundred percent of the cases of spiritually oppressed people we ministered to, the earliest recollection of trauma was an important means of entry for unclean spirits. This became such a reality to us that we made a guiding phrase out of it: *find the trauma and you will find the tormenting spirit.*

The goal of deliverance ministry is to first identify the spirits causing torment and harm, and then cast their defiling presence out. The more we can learn about how they gained entry, the more successful we can be in getting rid of their poison in a person's life.

TESTIMONY:
AN EARLY ENTRY OF TRAUMA THROUGH THE WOMB

The majority of demonic problems enter early in life, before people are able to respond to temptation and deal with trauma in a rational and thoughtful way. In fact, deliverance ministers quickly learn that numerous cases of demonic oppression begin while one is still in the mother's womb.

One such instance occurred with a man, Eli, who had spent 50 of his 57 years in and out of traumatic relationships. The door was opened to sexual addiction and torment through the trauma of a first sexual encounter at the *age of seven*. But the Holy Spirit had more to show us beyond what was on the surface for Eli. My wife, Eve, and I felt the prompting of the Spirit to look for another root to his problems. So, through a *word of knowledge* given at the time of ministry[2], the Spirit suggested we ask Eli about any earlier recollections; we sensed something had originated even earlier in his life. Specifically, we felt impressed upon us that a tormenting *spirit of rejection* had latched itself on to Eli when he was in his mother's womb.

As we mentioned this to him, his eyes lit up. Eli began to remember whispers from his past, hushed words spoken to him by an older sister long ago, while he was still quite young.

His sister had described to him a traumatic moment she witnessed when she saw their father hit their mother in the stomach while her brother Eli was in the womb. That violent act of rage and hate against the mother and the baby in her stomach, was all it took for the *spirit of rejection* to latch onto Eli and begin burrowing into him.

While this foothold of rejection had gained entry, Eli grew up in an environment exposed to even more rejection. His soul was

---

2   There are nine gifts of the Spirit mentioned in 1 Corinthians 12. A *Word of Knowledge* is one of these gifts and is often in operation during deliverance..

starved for love, and by the age of seven, predatory "wolves" entered his life and took advantage of him. This in turn left him more wounded, more confused of his true identity, and doubtful that love even existed.

When we began to address this root spirit of rejection in his life, his heart began to soften and become receptive to the love of Jesus Christ. The perfect love of Jesus casts out fear.

My wife and I ministered to him and commanded the *spirit of trauma* and *rejection* arising from the womb, and the *addiction to lust* that came from a traumatic sexual experience at the age of seven, to leave. We drove the unclean nature of those spirits away from Eli.

Praise Jesus, for there is always hope in Him.

TESTIMONY:
TRAUMA ATTACKS EARLY ON IN LIFE

A pastor asked my wife and I to minister to a young man recently released from jail to the custody of the pastor. The parolee had been charged with indecent exposure and public drunkenness, and was plagued by an addiction to drugs. We will call him Arthur, or "Art" for short.

After a bit of searching through his background, we learned that Art had experienced two traumatic experiences at an early age. Once while sitting in his father's car with his brother, and while looking at their front yard, his father came out of the house in a drunken frenzy holding a gun and pointing it at them wildly. His little soul had been traumatized, crushed that day by the thought of being murdered by his own parent, a father whom he relied upon for love and security.

The second trauma in his childhood was sexual in nature. His parents often left him and his brother in the custody of an older female cousin. While baby sitting with them, she would openly expose herself and perform lewd acts before them.

The experience of trauma at such a young age opened doors for evil spirits to harass Art for many years. There was a looming fear of death and violence coupled with the trauma of lust tormenting his soul. His addiction to drugs were the means to numb the pain from this spirit prowling his life. But that behavior led to more trauma in the form of fear of being punished.

As Art described, he became like a puppet on their string. In time these spirits caused him to act out in disturbing ways, and he became a social misfit.

We talked with Art about the source of his problems, and explained the root cause was first and foremost spiritual. He had received Jesus years ago, so we reconfirmed his commitment to the Lord and then prayed with him for deliverance. He agreed with us as we cast out the spirits by name, sealed the doors of his heart and mind against them by applying the blood of Jesus, and commanded them to cease their activity in him, in the name of Jesus Christ.

The Holy Spirit was present in a powerful way that day. With the help of the pastor and the church community, Art's way of life changed *dramatically* after that. In the months that followed, we saw him progress in wonderful ways. He grew as a born again Christian living in the Spirit of the Lord. He became heartedly employed and overcame his social awkwardness, resisting the *spirit of fear* and insecurity of his past as well as the route of escape through drugs. He became of sound mind. All this was for the glory of Jesus!

During counseling one day, Art asked an interesting question: why was his brother not affected in the way he was? After all, they were together at the time and had experienced the same trauma of seeing their father pointing a gun at them.

I asked the Lord for guidance on this, and His answer was clear.

The effect of trauma on a soul depends on the unique makeup of that soul. We each react to circumstances differently, both on a physical and a spiritual level. For Art, these experiences were traumatic, for his brother they were not as immediately destructive to his personality.

The truth was that his brother faced other issues as a result from the tragic episodes described. The damage done to Art's soul from trauma manifested differently than the damage done to the soul of his brother, but trauma had its effect in both cases.

TRAUMA BROUGHT ON BY BEING OVERWHELMED

Another door to trauma can come from being overwhelmed. If we strain or stretch our attention on too many matters, and fail to devote enough time to resting our heart on Jesus, demonic pressures will soon try to move in and overwhelm us. Their purpose is to traumatize us and drag us under. We begin to move further away from the cleansing righteousness of Jesus over us. Sin, sickness, oppression and other adversities try to convince us that God is not faithful or true.

The Apostles very wisely assigned some of their daily responsibilities, such as serving and distributing food, to deacons (Acts 6:2-4). This was done under the direction of the Holy Spirit who knows our need for rest.

Tithing includes time. God is entitled to some time with you each day because friendship and relationship is built on time and time often requires a sacrifice. Put God first and He will put you first.

> But seek ye first the kingdom of God, and his righteousness; and all these things shall be added unto you. Matt 6:33 KJV

Jesus tells us to ask, seek and knock (Matthew 7:7). Peter says we should grow in the spirit (2 Peter 3:18 AMPC.). Paul says to pray and even to sing in the spirit, as well as with understanding (1 Corinthians 14:15). Jude tells us to build ourselves up in our holy faith by praying in the Holy Spirit (Jude 20).

TESTIMONY:
NINA WAS A CHILD OF CONFLICT

Trauma can enter homes where young children witness strife and contention among their parents. Children of troubled marriages often experience such conflict in the home and this can be traumatic to their little souls. In the next case, a fellow deliverance minister, Bill Banks, describes how real the effect of trauma in the home can be on a young soul...

A young woman, a twenty-four year old school teacher named Nina, had previously received pray for deliverance from us. She was the product of much trauma: a broken home, a father who was an alcoholic, and a mother left destitute to support a family of three small children. When her father died while she was still young, she was left with feelings of being abandoned, and grieved over the loss of a relationship with him.

One evening, as she was visiting our home and prayerfully discussing the deliverance that she had already experienced, she said — quite suddenly — "I think I feel something else beginning to manifest!" The Lord began to work on her right then and there, seemingly out of the blue.

The Lord put His finger on a tormenting spirit and it began to cause her body to contort. I had not seen anything like this in the early years of our ministry; this was shocking to me.

As she sat in a chair in our family room, she began to curl up in a manner of crippling. Her legs twisted, her hands became claw-like, and her body was if it was in an advanced stage of paraplegia.

Then her body began to bend to the right. Her right shoulder came within a few inches of touching her right hip! Had I not witnessed it firsthand, I do not think I would have believed what was taking place. Five minutes earlier, as we were casually talking, no one would have suspected she had a problem requiring such incredible manifestation.

We commanded the crippling spirit to leave, and it did. Her muscles and joints returned to normal, and she returned to her normal posture. However, we sensed in the Spirit that there was something else present, so we commanded the next spirit to name itself and to come out. At this point, a guttural voice came out of her and shouted, "**CONFLICT!**" We commanded the spirit of conflict to come out of her, and she began to shake. As she was shaking, Nina began to cry out, "*I feel like I'm being pulled apart!*"

It is difficult to describe. She appeared as if she was being pulled apart at the shoulders, as if one person had hold of one arm and another the other arm, and were pulling her in opposite directions. Her shoulders looked as if they were going to be pulled out of their sockets! Then, as suddenly as it had come on, it was gone, and the battle was over. She was free.

She sat up and described what she felt was happening: "That was awful! I felt as if I was about to break in two, like I was going to be split right down the middle. When I was a child, and my parents fought, our house was filled with conflict. I felt like I was constantly being torn between them."

This spiritual bondage was directly related to the conflict she had experienced in her home as a child. It was a profound experience for us all.[3]

Similar to the trauma from conflict in a home and the inevitable

---

3   From the book *Deliverance for Children & Teens*, by Bill Banks. See the back of the book for more information.

tearing of divorce, when a child is put up for adoption, the little soul is often aware and even *on alert*.

A baby surrendered for adoption tends to occur in already troubled situations. Added to that, the abandonment of being placed in a new home without his or her parents is traumatic even if in an infant. We have ministered to many such cases, both children and grown adults, who experienced tremendous freedom after being set free from the trauma of abandonment from such an early time in their life.

Jesus is a mighty warrior to the oppressed, and has a special place in His heart for the fatherless.

> A father of the fatherless, a defender of widows, is God in His holy habitation.
> Ps 68:5

DELIVERANCE IS A MANDATE FROM HEAVEN

Hope comes from the manner in which Jesus dealt with unclean, tormenting spirits in Scripture. His will for us was forever established by the record of His earthly ministry. He spent a great deal of time casting out demonic, harassing spirits.

> At sunset, the people brought to Jesus all who had various kinds of sickness, and laying his hands on each one, he healed them. Moreover, **demons came out of many people**, shouting, "You are the Son of God!"
> Luke 4:40–41

Jesus demonstrated His will to cast out demons by doing it Himself. As He brought the light of Heaven, the darkness cried out and fled. But then He gave the commission to do the same to His twelve disciples.

> And they went out and preached that people are to repent. And they were casting out many demons
> Mark 6:12–13 NASB

Even with that, He did not stop there. Later in His ministry, He commissioned 72 of His followers to do the same.

> Now after this the Lord appointed seventy-two others... Now the seventy-two returned with joy, saying, **"Lord, even the demons are subject to us in Your name!"**
>
> Luke 10:1, 17

Then, to make absolutely sure we understood the seriousness and reality of the enemy we face, and the will of Jesus to drive out the defilement of these spirits, He commissioned the entire Church to engage in deliverance!

> And He said to them, "Go into all the world and preach the gospel to all creation... These signs will accompany those who have believed: **in My name they will cast out demons**
>
> Mark 16:15, 17

The very first sign Jesus said would accompany the preaching of the Kingdom would be the *casting out of unclean spirits.*

Do you think Jesus thought these spirits were real? Do you think He treated the subject with a consistency and an urgency? Would Jesus, the Good Shepherd of the sheep, tolerate evil trying to defile His flock? No, He would not! His earthly ministry showed us that freedom from bondage looks like, as He went about casting out spirits whenever He ministered to gatherings. He taught us how to break the hold of the *god of trauma*, Satan, and to open the doors of the prison house of our past.

> If the Son therefore shall make you free, ye shall be free indeed.
>
> John 8:36

Who among us deserves His gracious touch? Who among us has earned His miraculous intervention in our lives? None, we must admit. Yet He offers it to all freely and on an ongoing basis.

Heal the sick, raise the dead, cleanse those with leprosy, **cast out demons.** *Freely you received, freely give.* Matt 10:8 NASB

Deliverance becomes a mandate. Once you experience it, you want others to taste that freedom as well. The mission spreads, Heaven's light drives out more darkness, and the Kingdom expands. Freely we have received, so freely we can give to others.

The Lord knows the world in which we live is full of trauma and that evil seeks to take advantage of our fears. Therefore, He has made provision for deliverance to be an *ongoing* process:

He *has* **delivered us** from such a deadly peril, and **he** *will* **deliver us again.** On him we have set our hope that **he** *will continue* **to deliver us.** 2 Cor 1:10

That is deliverance for our past, our present and our future. Jesus considers deliverance a serious matter and He directs the resources of Heaven to assist us in getting this important work done. We have not been abandoned; we are not alone. Heaven us on our side!

Our need for deliverance is never greater than God's willingness and power to meet that need.

LONG DISTANCE DELIVERANCE: NO PROBLEM FOR OUR GOD

The will of God for our deliverance is so great that distance is not an issue. Many deliverances happen over the phone, even, since this important ministry is sorely lacking often in local communities. Phone deliverance can be an important first step as the Lord is not hindered by distance of any kind.

A woman we had been ministering to called on a Wednesday afternoon for prayer. Although it was right at supper time and the weather was bad, I discerned the need for more deliverance so I started to pray for her. But she stopped me. She insisted that I come back to her home right then but I refused.

I told her that evil spirits can be cast out over the phone, as I had witnessed many times. She disputed my statement. She insisted that I would have to lay hands on her for the demon to go. I told her the demon was gone, regardless of what she may have thought or believed. She made a few disgruntled statements and hung up the phone. The Lord proved us right later that evening.

That night she accompanied her family to a church they had never attended before. The pastor interrupted the service to call her out of the congregation. He said, "Sister, I have a word for you. The Lord would have me tell you that you are clean!"

In another case, a very young child called on the phone. Eve could not understand what he was saying and she did not recognize the voice. She assumed the child had dialed a wrong number but yet she still told him to call back later.

The child had called on behalf of his mother who could not hear well. The mother then went to a neighbor and had the neighbor call for her. She told Eve she was hearing voices and that she had discolored bruises on her body from spiritual attacks. Eve then prayed for her over the phone. I was on the extension supporting her with prayer in the spirit.

After Eve prayed I asked her how she felt. She said there was something in her throat and something was moving around in her body. Eve prayed again.

Then I asked her to put her neighbor back on the line. The neighbor described how this mother coughed violently and spit up something, and was calm after that. With that, she was free. Distance is not a problem in the power and the might of the Holy Spirit.

Matt 15:21-28

3

TRAUMA: AN OPEN DOOR
(FOR JESUS)

Trauma, as we have just seen, can be an open door for Satan and his infestation of evil spirits. Equally true, however, is that trauma can serve as an open door for Jesus. When Jesus enters through that door, He promises to turn our trauma into triumph.

Jesus longs to heal our broken hearts, and to bandage our wounds, in order to heal and restore us. This was true from the very first day of His ministry two thousand years ago. Consider the words Jesus spoke publicly, in a synagogue, at the start of His public ministry. Their meaning encapsulated the reason He was sent from Heaven; they are in essence His "mission statement."

> The Spirit of the Lord is upon me, because he hath anointed me to preach the gospel to the poor; **he hath sent me to heal the brokenhearted,** to preach **deliverance to the captives,** and... to [*free*] them that are bruised [*by chains and shackles*]...
>
> Luke 4:18, KJV

That is why Jesus came. Jesus came to save us, in more ways than one. This is born out when we consider the word used for salvation in the Old and New Testaments. But according to His own words, healing broken hearts, restoring damaged emotions and repairing traumatized minds was central to His mission to man.

SALVATION

There is a famous example of salvation that occurred on the shores of the Red Sea. When the armies of Egypt had cut off all avenues of escape for the Hebrew nation, and seeking vengeance for the death of their firstborn males, Moses stood before God's people and cried:

> "Do not be afraid. Stand still, and see the **salvation** [*yeshua*] of
> the Lord, which He will accomplish for you today."
>
> Ex 14:13

Yet to God's people that day, there was no way out. Their choice was trauma and death at the hands of the Egyptians, or to drown in the waters behind them. Salvation would have to come to them in the form of a mighty, miraculous deliverance. But we serve an infinitely creative, problem-solving, solutions-oriented God. Suddenly, God made a way; He made a way even where there was no way. The waters parted and the Hebrew nation escaped death while their seething enemies drowned in the Sea behind them.

In the Hebrew Moses spoke that day, "salvation" is the word *yeshua*. If one word had to summarize the miraculous parting of the Red Sea and the rescue of God's people from the molestation by their enemies, it would be this word. *Yeshua* meant they were saved from the traumatic situation in which they were trapped. *Yeshua* meant they were going to be delivered.

Why is this word *Yeshua* so significant? Because it meant deliverance from their enemies who sought to harm them. And…

Yeshua in the Old Testament is Jesus in the New Testament.

When the angel visited Mary to give her the good news, he told her the name she was to give her baby boy:

> And behold, you will conceive in your womb and give birth to a
> son, and you shall name Him **Jesus**.
>
> Luke 1:31, NASB

God chose the name for His Son. He chose to call Him Yeshua, or Jesus. Inextricably tied to that Name is the *promise of deliverance*. Written into the Name of the Son of God was His mission: to set free.

YESHUA BECOMES SOTERIA

At the Red Sea, Moses cried out to the people to stand still and see the *salvation* of their God. In the New Testament, we find the true fulfillment of the word for salvation.

> Jesus Christ the Nazarene... there is **salvation** [*soteria*] in no one else; for there is no other name under heaven that has been given among mankind by which we must be saved.
>
> Acts 4:10,12 NASB

In the Greek of the New Testament, salvation is *soteria*. There is a powerful, present application of the word for us today:

Soteria actually means deliverance

This is quite a word. It suggests deliverance from our sins and from the power of death, our way where there was no way into eternal life in the Kingdom of Heaven. That is important and true. But *soteria* is defined by Thayer's Lexicon[4] as "deliverance, preservation, safety and salvation." And, specifically with reference to deliverance, *soteria* means "deliverance from the molestation of enemies."

Jesus is our salvation, our *soteria*. This means Jesus came to "deliver us from the molestation of our enemies." Our battle, we are told by the Apostle Paul, is not against flesh and blood. So, who are our enemies that seek to molest us?

Of all the harassment and torment we have seen from the kingdom of Satan, through years of ministry to the oppressed, *fear* and *trauma* are among the greatest. These evil, unclean spirits are the enemies who seek to trap us on the shore of the Sea, to convince us we are cut off from God and without hope.

But then, out of nowhere, our problem-solving, miracle working God shows up and makes a way where there was no way. Jesus comes

---

4   *Thayer's Greek Lexicon*. J. H. Thayer.,1896

to us as the Great Deliverer.

God is fully aware that His choice of *soteria* includes a promise of not only deliverance from guilt and sin, but also deliverance from the molestation of spiritual enemies and foes. In fact,

He chose the Name for His Son, Yeshua or Jesus, to send this exact message.

GATES OF BRONZE, BARS OF IRON

Trauma can become an open door for Jesus to work the miraculous. When Jesus enters through that door, He fully intends to turn our trauma into our triumph.

Jesus has a plan for, and sees great potential, in each of us. When we are born-again, this potential is nothing short of greatness. Our God delights in taking the foolish things of the world to prove His glory to the wise and proud.

> But God hath chosen the foolish things of the world to confound the wise; and God hath chosen the weak things of the world to confound the things which are mighty; and base things of the world, and things which are despised, hath God chosen, yea, and things which are not, to bring to nought things that are...
>
> 1 Cor 1:27–29

Therefore, He enjoys revealing that potential for greatness within each of us.

A traumatized soul, however, is trapped in the pain and fear of the past. That soul is locked behind gates of bronze and bars of iron. That soul is in need of Jesus, because Jesus is a fighter and a rescuer. His will to fight is in His Name. As the Great Deliverer, He will not allow the enemy to stop Heaven's plan for us to achieve great things.

The deliverance ministry of Jesus, recorded in the Gospels, is evidence we need to know for sure that He will go to war and fight on our behalf. Isaiah we foretold of the ministry of deliverance, to unlock greatness, centuries before Jesus appeared:

> I will go before thee, and make the crooked places straight: I will **break in pieces the gates of brass, and cut in sunder the bars of iron**:
>
> And **I will give thee the treasures of darkness, and hidden riches of secret places**, that thou mayest know that I, the Lord, which call thee by thy name, am the God of Israel.
>
> Is 45:2–3, NKJV

Isaiah speaks of the will of Heaven to rescue us from prisons built around us through fear and trauma. Jesus is prepared to "break through gates of bronze" and "cut through bars of iron" in order to set us free from that prison. Now that sounds like a Great Deliverer to me!

The result of this war on our behalf will be the unveiling of the greatness that God sees within each of us. Isaiah calls this the "treasures of darkness" and the "riches stored in secret places." Where is that kind of treasure located?

> Those *treasures* **and** *riches* **are within you and I, waiting to be brought out of captivity and shown the light.**

God has placed that treasure in us. We do not have to perform some great act in our flesh to gain it, because the treasure is already there inside us, and it belongs to Him. He wants to bring this treasure out, and show it to the powers and principalities looking on.

> But we have this treasure in earthen vessels, that the excellence of the power may be of God and not of us.
>
> 2 Cor 4:7

It should be a great reassurance to know that Jesus not only knows our pain, but that He leans forward on His Throne in anticipation of defeating the work of the enemy in our lives.

> For this purpose the Son of God was manifested, **that he might destroy the works of the devil**.
>
> 1 John 3:8

JESUS STANDS READY, AT THE DOOR, TODAY

What is our role in this? Our role is to open the door and invite Him into our situation. Our role is to surrender our trauma to Him.

Jesus stands outside the door of our hearts and knocks, waiting for an invitation to be let in. What do we do in response? Invite Him in! This applies to salvation, but it also applies to His involvement in every issue in our life.

As a gentleman, He works by invitation. He does not break down the door to our hearts, or force His way across the threshold of our free will. He does not violate our personality. No, that is precisely what trauma does.

Rather, He waits for an open door. In setting this requirement for Himself,

> **Jesus has established Himself as the God who is the opposite of trauma.**

As He says to John in Revelation:

> **I stand at the door, and knock**: if any man hear my voice, and open the door, I will come in to him, and will sup with him, and he with me.
>
> Jesus, Rev 3:20

Jesus is the opposite of trauma. Trauma does not wait outside, it does not knock; it breaks the lock and forces its way in; it violates our space and our security. Trauma kicks in the door of our mind and heart, steals our peace and leaves us feeling abandoned, outside the Lord's protection.

When Jesus establishes His presence in our heart, there is security and there is stability.

I would like to give a few examples from the deliverance ministry of how removing the obstacle of trauma clears a path for triumph in our lives.

TESTIMONY:
KATHY & THE DEATH OF A RELATIVE [5]

One of the most obvious trauma-inducing moments is an experience with death. The trauma of hearing about a death can leave a wound deep inside. The last enemy Jesus will defeat is death itself. But for us, in the meantime, the wounds left from the shock can attract spiritual germs (demons) if these wounds are not attended to, after a normal period of grieving. Prolonged grief means a prolonged open wound.

And sometimes we are unaware of the trauma we carry inside from the shock of death. A fellow deliverance minister, Bill Banks, relates the following testimony.

A young woman named Kathy came to visit one afternoon and said, "My problem is kind of strange. I have dated very few times in my life, although I am 27. I get extremely nervous before I go on a date." She continued, "I agree to go out with someone, and then I hate the thought of going and even become physically ill." She concluded, "I don't think that's natural."

I agreed, it did not seem natural. She had at one point even attempted suicide because of being overwhelmed by her sense of feeling abnormal. Her sisters had all dated normally and were all married, as was her brother. So this issue was unique to Kathy.

She told me, "I do want to get married: I want to have a normal life. My goal is to be married and have children, but I just absolutely

---

5   From the book, *Deliverance for Children & Teens* by Bill & Sue Banks. See the back of the book for more information.

panic at the thought of a date."

We spent half an hour searching for any hint of a problem from her past, including rejection, or sexual abuse, or any variation of being mistreated by a member of the opposite sex. But, after all that searching, we found nothing to speak of. No one in her family had experienced divorce; there were no broken marriages in her immediate family. We were at a loss for the root of this spiritual harassment in her life.

Even more telling, she had no problems being around men she did not consider a potential date. "I get along fine with all the men at work," she noted, where there was no pressure to bring her emotional attachment into the situation.

Stumped as we were, we decided to take a moment and wait on the Lord. As we sat in silence, her face lit up with revelation. She was suddenly reminded of a moment of trauma in her life.

"Something just came to my mind as we were waiting on the Lord to speak. I don't understand what it has to do with any of this. But I remember that when I was a child of five or six, my aunt came to our house unannounced, and in a state of panic. She told my mother about the death of their brother, one of my uncles, who had been killed in the Vietnam War."

Tears started to well up in Kathy's eyes. It was obvious that she had been deeply hurt by this loss, but had buried it out of fear of adding to the distress of her mother over the loss of that loved one. A fear of some kind had entered at this point in her childhood related to the death of a relative.

I asked if she had known him well, and she said, "Yes, although I was so young that he was more of someone I knew my mother cared about." It came to the surface during our prayer time that the fear of losing a loved one had been the root of the anxiety in her personal life. Kathy had been traumatized, as a little child, by seeing and experiencing the hurt that her mother suffered over the loss of Kathy's uncle.

With the root to her problems exposed, we were able to pray effectively for her deliverance from the trauma and fear of becoming emotionally bonded to a man in her life.

TESTIMONY:
FEAR OF LOOMING DEATH OR HARM

There are many examples of torment from Satan's kingdom latching onto a soul through trauma in early, childhood. In some cases, it is not the death of another person that causes trauma but a real threat of death to the child himself.

A mother described how her husband, in a drunken stupor, threw her baby son at a wall. A relative in the room miraculously caught the infant in midair, or his life would have been snuffed out as soon as he hit the wall with such great force. The son, Zach, grew up with the effects of this trauma and now, at the age of 25, his mother was seeking the ministry of deliverance for her son.

During our ministry to Zach, it was learned that the father tried the same thing again when he was five years old. Twice the boy's life had come close to death. These traumatic encounters with bodily harm, and even potential death, opened spiritual doors in Zach's fragile young mind which led, eventually, to the entry of tormenting spirits of mental illness in Zach's life.

How evil were these spirits? One cannot fully comprehend the evil that originates with Satan and his kingdom. Apparently these voices of trauma had tormented him so severely in his mind that he had a series of mental breakdowns, and had been admitted to mental hospitals three times.

To add to his grief, Zach was unable to stay for long in a church setting, the one place that would have allowed him refuge from the voices of torment, especially during praise and worship. He could not sit still for long in that environment because the voices spoke vile, blasphemous accusations against those around him. And by the time the message began, these lying, deceiving spirits would terribly distort the intent and meaning of the message being preached.

In our first ministry session with Zach, my wife Eve and I identified the root stronghold, or what Jesus called the *spiritual strongman*, and cast it out. That opened the floodgates of Heaven, and both he and his mother received the *baptism in the Holy Spirit* (as described in Acts 2)[6] and both rejoiced in their new prayer language as they spoke in tongues. With this new language, their "warfare language," they were armed to confront the enemy following our initial session.

The Holy Spirit edifies, which means He builds us up and strengthens us in the areas of our life where we need it most. Depending on our circumstances, this could include our physical body, our mind and thought life, and our emotional health.

Speaking in tongues has a powerful effect in the life of a believer that many do not understand. As a warrior language, the act of faith of speaking in tongues cleanses the spiritual environment around us; demons hate the sound of tongues because it is a language of pure faith; it takes faith to speak it! Tongues also have the effect of ushering us (quickly) into the presence of the Lord. Thus,

the act of speaking tongues, in faith, allows a mighty work to happen within us in a spiritually cleansed environment.

I like to compare speaking in tongues to the effort taken to prepare

6   Refer to the booklet on the baptism in the Holy Spirit entitled *Promoted by God*, by Frank Hammond. See the back of the book for more information.

an operating room for surgery. Great care has to be taken to eliminate germs that may come into the room on the flesh of those who enter. Those germs will get in the way of the careful work of the surgeon and cause complications to the patient. Thus, effort is required to create an environment in a surgical room to render it as undefiled as possible. In the same way, speaking in tongues cleanses the atmosphere around us of spiritual defilement (demonic harassment) and the presence of God makes itself known in a tangible way. Then the Great Physician can operate without interruption, on our minds and on our hearts and, like a surgeon, begin to remove the shrapnel left in us from the traumatic episodes of our life.

This is why the devil hates speaking in tongues so much, and why he causes people (even within the church) to hate those who step out in faith in such ways. In fact, as you consider all the spiritual gifts mentioned in 1 Corinthians 12, each has a role in bringing glory to Jesus and taking control away from Satan. I urge all to find a quiet place away from the ears of others to practice the presence of God, through the vocal gift of speaking in tongues. This is what Zach and his mother realized they needed to do for the cleansing of their home, and the strengthening of Zach's mind.

Speaking in tongues for Zach opened other avenues for the Holy Spirit to work in his life. When they returned for a second session, Zach told of a spiritual dream he had been given the night before. He had a dream about his biological father, the abuser who had been out of his life for many years. Zach was moved by this dream, and I felt led to pray for the Spirit to reveal its significance.

What the Spirit revealed was that an overriding sense of guilt had been placed on Zach. Although the father was unquestionably guilty of all sorts of physical, verbal and mental abuse, the boy blamed himself. He was the one being tortured, mentally, by a demonic spirit of guilt even though he had done nothing wrong, as is the case so often with victims of domestic abuse. The dream was the instrument the Holy Spirit used to expose this stubborn enemy that weighed on his mind, guilt.

Guided by the Spirit, we were able to show him how the father was the guilty party, not Zach. The interpretation of the dream helped him understand this, and a light of self-esteem began to shine in his eyes.

The young man at this time was still hearing voices, but he was coping with them through that gift of tongues. He may not have known it, but we did: he was flexing spiritual muscles and the spiritual forces looking on were taking notice. They were losing their power. Ushering in the presence of the Holy Spirit through speaking in tongues had been an effective method of cleansing the spiritual atmosphere around him, even though the battle was still being waged.

But, while we were ministering and waiting on the Lord, a remarkable thing happened. The Holy Spirit spoke to me. He said "tell that young man to stop listening to the voices and to listen to Me!"

This was a breakthrough moment for Zach. I asked him to pray for interpretation of his own tongues, as the Apostle Paul says we can (1 Corinthians 14:13). Zach did, excited to know this was even a possibility.

He then spoke in tongues, with only two words of interpretation in English. But those two words were so faith-filled, they were the beginning of his victory over the lying voices of the enemy that had plagued him for decades.

Two sessions later this young man was like a new person, full of confidence and full of hope for the future. Praise the Lord!

4

THE BIBLE AS A RECORD OF PEOPLE IN TRAUMATIC SITUATIONS

A significant amount of trauma exists in modern society. After countless wars mixed with oppressive regimes, hundreds of millions have been traumatized, and a *spirit of trauma* has invaded generational family lines across the world.

As if daily life wasn't challenging enough, make-believe invades our minds through the media. Our entertainment industry earns big bucks from traumatizing audiences who willingly pay for the thrill of being terrified, leaving them emotionally drained. This constant feast of psychological trauma weighs heavily on the human mind and soul. What we watch and what we listen to affects our heart, our mind and our ability to rest in the goodness of God. When real trauma strikes, we are not prepared because we are already living with the consequences of Hollywood-induced trauma.

God has an answer. He wants to entertain us with what *He* is capable of doing. He wants to show us what He can do in the lives people facing trauma. We have God-given, real life stories of traumatic experiences that have uplifted and influenced people for thousands of years. They are available collectively in book form, known as the *Bible*.

THE BIBLE AND TRAUMA

Trauma is not new to humanity. We find instances of it throughout the lives of the men and women recorded in the Bible. In fact,

one of the main reasons we remember the men and women of the Bible so well is because they were subjected to traumatic experiences, and came out of them triumphantly.

Traumatic experience was what *qualified* these men and women to have their stories recorded for all the world to read.

What makes Biblical characters so unique is that so many were subjected to extreme pressure of some kind, and that level of pressure was traumatic. They triumphed over pressure, and over the trauma of their situation, because the presence of the Lord was with them. God wants us to know the same is possible for us today.

When we read what they went through, it puts our traumatic experiences in perspective. Hebrews 11 provides a list of some of the more serious encounters with pressure and the traumatic experiences of the people of God. Some of our Biblical heroes...

> ... were tortured, not accepting deliverance, that they might obtain a better resurrection. Still others had trial of mockings and scourgings, yes, and of chains and imprisonment. They were stoned, they were sawn in two, were tempted, were slain with the sword. They wandered about in sheepskins and goatskins, being destitute, afflicted, tormented—of whom the world was not worthy. They wandered in deserts and mountains, in dens and caves of the earth.
>
> Heb 11:35–38

So admirable were they in Heaven's eyes that "the world was not worthy" of their presence. Yet, they were men and women just like us. Take Elijah for instance,

> Elijah was a man with a nature like ours...
>
> James 5:17 NKJV

His story and the stories of those we draw encouragement from in Scripture are there to spur us on:

> The effective, fervent prayer of a righteous man avails much.
>
> James 5:16 NKJV

Trauma does not exclude us from achieving greatness; when we welcome Jesus to become involved, trauma can be the very thing that propels us toward accomplishing great things in our life, like the Biblical heroes of old.

We do not ask for trauma. God does not send it. No, the enemy of our soul, the *god of this present age*, sends it. But when it comes, we can be assured that Jesus has a plan to turn it around for our good and to turn our trauma into triumph:

> And we know that all things work together for good to those who love God...
>
> Rom 8:28 NKJV

It is not whether we face trauma in life that matters, for most if not all humans will, at some point. What matters is how we respond. When we turn to God as our source during these dark times of uncertainty and testing, He will, in His perfect timing, turn our mess into a miracle, our test into a testimony.

TRAUMATIC SITUATIONS IN JOSEPH'S LIFE

The life of Joseph is perhaps one of the best examples of an encounter with trauma. While favored by his father Jacob, Joseph was hated by his brothers. His own family inflicted the wounds of rejection and hatred against him. This hatred against him grew to such an extent that his brothers tried to murder him, deciding at the last moment to instead sell him into slavery to foreigners.

Can we imagine the effect this would have had on a young lad? Joseph was abandoned by his own kin and sold by those who were supposed to have loved him and cared for him *the most!*

Once in Egypt, the Lord proved that He was with him and Joseph quickly gained recognition for his diligence. He was put in charge of Potiphar's entire household, Potiphar being the captain of the royal guard of Pharaoh (the king of Egypt). But before long, as if lighting could strike twice in the same place, Joseph was falsely accused of sexual abuse by Potiphar's wife and thrown into prison with no hope of ever seeing freedom. Languishing in prison and without a path forward, he was subjected to the trauma of the uncertainty of outcome, including the possibility of death behind bars. And, for the second time, trauma came for no fault of his own.

God's favor appeared again to Joseph, even in prison. As he showed diligence in his routine, the keeper of the prison took notice and placed him in charge of running it in a righteous manner.

> And the keeper of the prison committed to Joseph's hand all the prisoners who were in the prison; whatever they did there, it was his doing.
>
> Gen 39:22

God did not leave Joseph as a slave in Egypt, nor as a prisoner in a dungeon. God eventually turned all this traumatic experience into glory. Joseph was released, becoming *second to the king*, Pharaoh, and ruled over all the pagan land!

> "Inasmuch as God has shown you all this, there is no one as discerning and wise as you. You shall be over my house, and all my people shall be ruled according to your word; only in regard to the throne will I be greater than you." And Pharaoh said to Joseph, "See, I have set you over all the land of Egypt."
>
> Gen 41:39–41 NKJV

God even provided Joseph with a good woman, a lady named Asenath to be his wife, in a land that did not know the Lord. Throughout Joseph's life, God was always bigger than the circumstances at hand.

Joseph was able to look back on the long list of encounters with trauma and conclude that God was faithful to him through it all. Even more, God took the trauma and turned it into Joseph's triumph. The names Joseph chose for his children express this sense of triumph over the trauma he faced:

> Joseph called the name of the firstborn *Manasseh*: **"For God has made me forget all my toil and all my father's house."** And the name of the second he called *Ephraim*: **"For God has caused me to be fruitful in the land of my affliction."**
>
> Gen 41:51–52

God had apparently caused the blessing in Joseph's life to be so great that he looked beyond the abandonment by his brothers, and the affliction he went through in an Egyptian prison through false accusation. Every time the enemy tried to bring trauma against Joseph, God would reverse it and bring Joseph out on a higher level of abundance in the land. Joseph was able to speak a version of Romans 8:28 to his brothers at the end of the matter, even thousands of years before it was written. That which was meant for harm, God had turned around for not only his good but the good of his entire family." In the words of Paul,

> And we know that God causes all things to work together for good to those who love God, to those who are called according to His purpose.
>
> Rom 8:28, NASB

Now that is a promise to hold on to! God did that for Joseph, a man just like us. What can he do for you and I?

SAUL, THE FIRST KING OF ISRAEL, UNDER PRESSURE

While many Biblical characters are remembered for how they overcame trauma, a few are remembered by how it overcame them. Saul, the first anointed king of Israel, is one example.

The first King of Israel, Saul, was confronted with a traumatic decision, and his life changed dramatically for the worse from that time on. A prophet of God (Samuel) warned him not to lead his army out against the enemy until a sacrifice had been offered. Samuel, the anointed representative of God, was authorized to perform the sacrifice, but King Saul had to wait for him to return. Samuel said he would be gone for seven days (1 Samuel 10:8).

When seven days had gone by and Samuel was nowhere to be seen, pressure came over Saul. It was decision time. The enemy was before him ready to attack (1 Samuel 13:5). His people were fearfully departing. Some hid in caves, some followed him trembling, and others deserted him altogether (1 Samuel 13:6-8).

The pressure led Saul to sense rejection, stirring something deep inside him. In response to a perceived rejection by Samuel, he became impatient, angry and irreverent. In an act of rebellion against God, the king performed the sacrifice himself, even though Samuel had made clear he was not to. And guess what happened? As soon as he completed the sacrifice, Samuel arrived.

The prophet charged him with foolish disobedience (1 Samuel 13:10-13). This decision by Saul, in a time of pressure and traumatic testing, brought a deep sense of guilt and paranoia into his life. Evil spirits of *torment, rage, jealousy, anger, hatred, murder, depression, confusion* and *self-destruction* began to manifest. King Saul was for the first time without the support and discipline of God's influence in his life, and the king's nature changed for the worse.

Today, we are living in world of Saul, but we have access to God's mighty delivering hand through His Holy Spirit. Both the tools of discipline and the power of deliverance are freely available to us, so that we do not have to live in bondage to unclean spirits like King Saul. *Thank you Jesus!*

DANIEL AND HIS FRIENDS
FACED TRAUMA IN A FOREIGN LAND

The capture of Israel by King Nebuchadnezzar of Babylon, the burning of the Temple, and the forced exodus into a pagan land were traumatic events for God's people. Included in the throngs of captives were Daniel and his colleagues, men who were forced to serve in the pagan court of the King. The enemy's wish against them was ever-present in their lives, it seems and this led to a number of well know traumatic experiences.

When faced with the impossible choice to bow down to the King's idol or face a gruesome death, Shadrach, Mesach and Abednego chose to stand for their God. They knew full well the consequences of taking their stand for the Lord, and despite the extreme social pressure and risk to their lives, they chose the furnace over worshipping the idol.

These men not only stood up to trauma, they stared back at it and got in its face! They fought the threat and trauma of fear when they were thrown into the fiery furnace, heated so hot that the soldiers around them burned alive. Jesus appeared to them in the midst of the trauma and flames of the furnace:

> Then King Nebuchadnezzar was astonished; and he rose in haste and spoke, saying to his counselors, "Did we not cast three men bound into the midst of the fire?" They answered and said to the king, "True, O king." "Look!" he answered, "I see four men loose, walking in the midst of the fire; and they are not hurt, and the form of the fourth **is like the Son of God.**"
>
> Dan 3:24–25, NKJV

These men emerged from their furnace with a testimony. Not only were their ropes and chains burned off, they did not even have the smell of smoke on them. God turned their a potentially traumatic situation into a triumph and their story is recorded for us today. Yet Shadrach, Meshach and Abednego were men just like us today.

DANIEL AND THE LIONS' DEN

Daniel was also subjected to pressure. He was skilled in administration and became highly favored to the point of being *second to the king in all the land.* But his hard work created enemies who were threatened by his favor and success. As a result, they devised a trap to force Daniel to choose between worshiping His God or obeying the king. When he chose to worship God, he was imprisoned and sentenced to death in a lion's den.

To us today, the prospect of being eaten alive by starving lions would be traumatic, right? Daniel was a man just like us. Daniel had an active spiritual life and was secure in the Lord. He refused to give up his discipline of worship and prayer three times a day. Because of this routine, Daniel was well acquainted with his God, and one of the most prepared of all the saints for the traumatic experiences ahead. He was so familiar with his God that he had successfully tuned out the voice of trauma shouting "death!" even as he was being lowered into a pit with lions.

Acquaint now thyself with him, and be at peace...   Job 22:21

The pit with lions represents the very nature of trauma. Daniel emerging from the pit of lions represented the perfect triumph over trauma.

When Daniel emerged from the pit, he did so without a scratch. He was restored, and he prospered again as second in all the land. God shut the mouths' of the lions and turned Daniel's encounter with a traumatic situation into his triumph, recorded for us. And Daniel was a man just like us.

ESTHER FACED POTENTIAL TRAUMA

Esther was a captive of the Babylonian invasion into Israel. She lived with her uncle Mordecai in Susa, the capital of Persia.

Growing up in a foreign land as a second-class citizen would have been traumatic for most people. But then she was forcibly taken from her uncle and placed in the court of the foreign King as he searched for a suitable bride. God put so much favor on Esther that not only was she chosen as the Queen of all of Persia, but her Godly character impacted the King greatly and affected the entire empire. Despite all the uncertainty in her life, she did not leave the God of her hope and the God of hope never left her.

Still more trauma awaited her, however. A man rose to prominence in the King's court and convinced the King to slaughter her people. Imagine the trauma of learning that everyone you knew and cared about, as well as millions of others from your homeland, were about to be murdered through genocide. Added to this stress was that, by law, Esther could not enter the presence of the King to plead for the lives of her people; she had to be summoned instead. Were she to violate this rule, she herself could have been executed. She was in a lose-lose situation with no way out.

Trauma tries to blind us to the hope we have in God. It strips us of our sense of security because the fires of affliction and pressure rage around us. In some cases, panic ensues. Esther may have shown signs of stress as she wrestled through this time of decision. We could imagine a lack of appetite, loss of sleep, perhaps even outbursts of tears, irritability and anger. We don't know for sure, but we do know she was under a great deal of pressure and faced with the distressing loss of her entire people including her uncle Mordecai. What we do know is that Esther was human just like us.

The Queen persevered. She did the one thing she knew to do and that was to call a fast. As she and those in her community petitioned the Lord, she prepared herself to face certain death by entering the presence of the King. The purposes of the Lord prevailed, the enemy of her people was led to the gallows, and her faithfulness to intervene on her people's behalf earned her a unique title among women that stands to this day.

All this achievement in Esther's life came not because of the absence of pressure and trauma, but through it. God showed Himself strong on her behalf and proved to her, and to us today through her, that no situation is too big or too traumatic for Him. God turned her encounter with trauma into triumph, and with it the triumph of millions of people whose lives were spared.

God's will today is the same as it was in the days of Joseph, Esther, Daniel and so many others. Jesus will take the worst the enemy sends against us and turn it around for our good, if we invite Him into our circumstances and allow Him to work.

Like His Father, Jesus is a problem-solving, solutions-oriented God.

THE HEROES OF OLD

We could talk of traumatic experiences in the Bible all day! We have only scratched the surface in this chapter. We could, for instance, talk about the traumatic experiences of the prophet Jeremiah who was severely hated (and had death threats against him) for speaking the truth of God to a Jerusalem under siege; and how he wound up imprisoned at the bottom of a well without food or water, facing imminent death. Or we could speak of Nehemiah, a man tasked to rebuild the defensive walls of Jerusalem while under attack by his enemies. He had to have his men build the wall with one arm and carry a weapon in the other!

We could also talk of those in the New Testament who faced

traumatic experiences, like the parents of Jesus who learned King Herod was intent on killing the young children in the land, and they had to flee to a foreign land, Egypt.

We could also talk about the trauma Paul was subjected to when he was shipwrecked, lost at sea for days! Or after finding refuge on an island, being bitten by a poisonous viper in the campfire on shore.

We tend to read these familiar stories with a stoic attitude, ignoring the very real, heart racing and dizzying effect the attack of trauma had on all these men and women.

They were called to be examples for us today. They are examples for us to not give in, and to not give up hope. While we may battle with despair, we are not to surrender to it. We must wait on the Lord Jesus for His Hand to rescue, to preserve, to resolve and to restore. Hope comes to us knowing that much of His work happens behind the scenes as we are unaware.

THE TRAUMA OF JESUS

Most important of all, we could talk about the trauma that came against Jesus. He had to ensure the harshest form of rejection, because it came from the very people for whom His Father had cared and provided for over a thousand years. Rejection and abuse by His own people included being called a "false prophet," a "blasphemer," even "demon-possessed."

Abusive words alone can be traumatic. But then He was turned over by His own people to the ruthless pagan authorities who ruled the land. He was to be brutally flogged, and sentenced to a criminal's death even though He was an innocent man.

Do you know there has only been one sinless man in all history, and that was Jesus? Yet He had to walk through the fires of traumatic attacks against him.

In all His distress, Jesus did not allow Satan to damage His soul, or to lessen His faith in the goodness of His Father.

As time approached for Jesus to face the Cross, the thought of the brutal treatment ahead and of being made sin for the world began to weigh heavily on His soul, and He came under tremendous pressure:

> "Father, if You are willing, remove this cup from Me; yet not My will, but Yours be done." ... And **being in agony**, He was **praying very fervently**; and His sweat became like drops of blood, falling down upon the ground.
>
> Luke 22:42, 44 NASB

This was the ultimate traumatic experience for Jesus, as He prepared Himself for what He was about to go through on our behalf. In His moment of distress, He was in "agony" but He faced it by seeking God's will and praying fervently. His heavenly Father, compassionate and gracious, full of mercy and loving-kindness, responded by sending an angel to strengthen Him.

> Now **an angel from heaven** appeared to Him, **strengthening Him**.
>
> Luke 22:43

God was with Jesus in His encounter with extreme trauma and poured out His heart for His Son. God sent an angel, a mighty angel, to appear to Jesus and to strengthen Him in His hour of need.

Jesus stands above the rest as a model for our trauma-filled lives. Even in the worst moment of His life, He knew to cry out to the Father for help and to pray. The Father responded and strengthened Him. Jesus, despite the craziness around Him, the attacks of rage coming against Him, and the task before Him (the Cross), remained stable in His soul and untouched by Satan in His soul. He did this through His connection to His Father in Heaven.

> For it was fitting for us to have such a high priest, holy, innocent, **undefiled**
>
> Heb 7:26

Jesus, through prayer and cries to the Father, remained undefiled.

The Father took the encounter with the Cross and turned the greatest of all traumatic experiences into the greatest of all triumphs.

God turned it around for our good by opening a door to eternal life. He turned it around for our good by releasing the power and might of the Holy Spirit, the Counselor and Comforter, to be with us in our tribulations. God also turned it around for our good by giving us a High Priest in Heaven, Jesus, who is well acquainted with our trials and suffering.

But as a proud Father, God turned it around for the good of His Son by setting Jesus on the throne in Heaven.

> ... who for the joy set before Him endured the cross, despising the shame, and **has sat down at the right hand of the throne of God**.
>
> Heb 12:2, NASB

Knowing that we, too, would have to face traumatic experiences, He set Jesus on the throne of mercy and grace to meet with us in our time of need:

> For we do not have a high priest who cannot sympathize with our weaknesses, but One who has been tempted in all things just as we are, yet without sin.
>
> Therefore let's approach the throne of grace with confidence, **so that we may receive mercy and find grace for help at the time of our need**.
>
> Heb 4:15

As the Father gave mercy and favor to His Son, the Son now gives mercy and favor to us.

Lastly, God turned the Cross around for our good by granting us the right to reign with Jesus in the ages to come. If we endure the firs of trauma, we will also reign with His Son:

> If we endure, we will also reign with Him
>
> 2 Tim 2:12, NASB

TRAUMATIC SITUATION CAN BECOME OUR TRIUMPH

As you study God's Word, you will become keenly aware that the reason the men and women recorded in Scripture stand out, the reason they are so easily impressed upon our memory, is because trauma played a large role in their stories. God gave us the stories of these precious men and women to know that while trauma may be a the pit that we are pushed into, we can emerge unscathed and better off because the mighty Hand of the Lord is with us. Trauma can be a precursor to our triumph.

The record of their lives, and the redemption of their situations by Heaven on their behalf, is a constant lesson that needs to be learned and relearned as we journey through our own traumatic experiences in life. Nothing is too great for our God, and He longs to come aside us to work His problem-solving, healing work.

Whether we are living in good, peaceful times or in dark times of trauma:

- God is a problem-solving, solutions-oriented God who enjoys getting into the thick of things and facing our challenges alongside us.

- God seeks to alleviate our suffering while at the same time working things out for our good (Rom 8:28), if we allow Him into our situations.

- God will make a way when there is no way.

5

RESIST FEELINGS
OF REJECTION BY GOD

We have just learned that what Satan intended as a weapon of trauma can become God's weapon for our triumph. However, trauma is a thief with many disguises. In some cases, the thief sneaks into our lives through the shock and wound of rejection by those around us. When this happens, it is critical to the health our soul to resist interpreting rejection by man as rejection originating from God.

THE DOOR OF REJECTION

Rejection is one of the most common spirits Satan uses to harass and stunt our spiritual growth. Most people in need of deliverance come with a mix of fear of rejection or the trauma of having being rejected in some form.

Rejection is not new to modern man, but we do live in an increasingly critical world. Social media gives everyone a voice to criticize others, if they so choose.

Young people today are subjected to exponential amounts of rejection if they pay attention to the criticism swirling online. Imagine if you were to see photos from all the birthday parties you weren't invited to in your school-age years; that is normal life for kids today. The mere exclusion from gatherings can translate into rejection and poke like a knife in the heart of a young person.

Rejection is real and it is everywhere. But at the same time, perceived rejection is also real. Perceived rejection can create trauma in our hearts as much as real rejection, except it is a phantom; a lie. Perceptions are mental games the enemy plays to get into our minds and control our view of reality. Unclean spirits will make us think we are being rejected when we aren't. Some people who come for ministry are there because perceptions have overruled reality. While they do have a spiritual problem, it is not so much with rejection as it is with the *perception of rejection, low self esteem,* and the expectation of rejection which can lead to a *spirit of paranoia.*

With that being said, rejection is often the first tormenting spirit people encounter in life. In fact, as we have shown, rejection can even occur while a baby is in the womb. In another example, we have had cases of people come in for ministry who knew their mother had attempted an abortion against them, but failed to carry through. These tormented souls carried a *spirit of rejection* and a *fear of being murdered* for years because of it.

Rejection can also start early outside the womb in the case of an unwanted birth, strife in the home, or through sibling rivalry. There really are limitless ways the enemy can use this weapon to create traumatic experiences to wound people's souls and to stunt our spiritual growth. Yet...

> **In all these instances, rejection is being directed against us by man, not by God.**

SATAN'S LIE

When we experience rejection by others, it is a common mistake to assume it is coming from God. This is a product of our collective expulsion from the Garden as humans, to see every form of rejection as coming ultimately from Heaven itself.

> **One of the greatest lies hoisted on man since he first set foot outside the Garden is to believe that rejection by man is really rejection by God.**

It is not coincidental that Satan used "perceived rejection" to lead the first man and woman to rebel against God and get thrown out of the Garden in the first place. He asked Eve, "Did God really say you couldn't eat? Would a God who loves you really deny you food? Are you sure He loves you the way He says He does? Why would He deny you the opportunity of becoming wise like a god?"

It was all lies, but the distorted, false perception of reality became more dangerous than reality itself. Eve acted on the basis of those false perceptions, Adam followed suit, and their actions lead to consequences for all mankind. It was not reality, it was the false perception of reality. It was a lie.

If perceived rejection can have such a traumatic effect, imagine the traumatic effect real rejection can have, especially among the young, and the lingering *fear of rejection* that results.[7]

DAVID CRIES OUT FOR CLARITY IN PSALM 86

David spoke directly to this plague of perceived rejection by God in Psalm 86. His words in this Psalm are a cry to the Most High God from a troubled soul dealing with extreme rejection.

In the midst of traumatic threats of harm against him by men bent on his destruction, David cries out to God:

> God, arrogant men have risen up against me, and a gang of violent men have sought my life
>
> Ps 86:14, NASB

This experience for David was as real him as it is for some of us today. "Violent, ruthless, arrogant" men were attacking him. What was their goal? Nothing short of killing him.

David did not claim he was innocent or not to blame for the attacks; he is silent on the matter. Was it his fault? Was he innocent? We do not know. But as a child of God, David knew the throne of

---

7   Refer to *Overcoming Rejection* by Frank & Ida Mae Hammond. Also *Rejection - The Spiritual Cause* on Audio CD. See the back of the book for more information..

God was the place to seek counsel and clarity. First, however, David had to overcome a subtle, lingering fear that God was in someway behind these men.

In essence, David is wondering:

> **"God there are ruthless, violent men after me. They hate me. Is this coming from you? Are you finally done with me? Have I upset you so much that these ruthless men now represent Your will towards me? Have you sent these men to show that You have finally rejected me?"**

That is the burning question in many minds when faced with the rejection and ruthlessness of others. Who sent these men? Was it the God of Heaven?

David had to wrestle his brain out of the traumatic fog of not knowing the source of the attack. He had to address the pressing thought in his mind as to whether this aggression had been sent by God.

David resolves this dilemma by making a proclamation:

> God, arrogant men have risen up against me, and a gang of violent men have sought my life... [but] **they have not set You before them**.
>
> Ps 86:14, NASB

David proclaims, *but* "they have not set You before them." With that short phrase the entire stronghold of doubt being setup in his mind comes tumbling down. How was he able to do this? How did he manage to clear his mind even while he was in the fiery trial?

David reminded himself of who his God really is.

While David was not perfect, these men were ruthless, violent and arrogant. Thus, they could not be operating under the direction of Heaven, because they had nothing to do with God. Rather, the aggressive, violent, ruthlessness of their nature speaks to the god of rejection, Satan, instead.

This was an empowering moment for David in the midst of his traumatic experience.

David comes to a powerful conclusion by contrasting the nature of these men to the nature of His God. He continues:

[Because] You, O Lord, **are a God full of compassion, and gracious, longsuffering and abundant in mercy and truth.**

Do you see the contrast David has just established in his mind? These ruthless, violent, prideful men are the direct opposite of the nature of God. That description above is the God that David has come to know and serve. David knew His God!

- The God of Heaven is "compassionate," these men, however, are not. These men are vindictive and ruthless.

- God is "gracious," but these men are void of all grace.

- God is "patient and longsuffering." Not so these men; they have lost their mind with rage. They are after David's destruction, and as fast as possible.

- God is abundant in "mercy, truth and love." Love, mercy and truth are completely absent from the men coming against David, men who are ruthless, aggressive, violent and arrogant.

Divine nature stands in opposition to the nature and will of the ruthlessness of this world. Know your God and you will know the source of rejection in your life is not coming from Him.

Here is the power of David's revelation. If these men were not acting in accordance with the character of God, then they were not acting in line with the will of God. If they were not acting in line with the will of God then they were acting *against* the will of God. If they were acting against the will of God then they were enemies of righteousness, and in that sense, enemies of God. Thus, David could declare *"but these men have not set You before them."*

And, if God was not on their side, God is available to be on David's side. There was hope! Amen and Amen.

Through reminding himself of who God really is, David was able to re-establish his faith in his acceptance by God. He was able to resist the traumatic thought that God was somehow behind this ruthless, violent attack sent to reject him and to kill him.

David was therefore able to stabilize in God's love.

With his feet firmly back on solid ground, David could pray for deliverance from these attacks by invoking Heaven to work on his behalf. And that is the power of the contrast David set for us in Psalm 86. That is a powerful revelation we can with us for the rest of our lives because God's character does not change!

After years of believing the voice inside your head that says otherwise, you may not yet be convinced that God is really as good as David describes Him here. After all, David sounds like he is being over-enthusiastic, you might think. Thankfully, he is not the only person in the Bible to present God in this light.

You, O Lord, **are a God full of compassion, and gracious, longsuffering and abundant in mercy and truth.**

This definition of God shows up in Exodus, Nehemiah and throughout other Psalms. It was even spoken by Jonah when God saved Nineveh. Take a look at how many times this description of God is repeated in the Bible:

- Exodus 34:6
- Nehemiah 9:17
- Psalm 86:15
- Psalm 103:8
- Psalm 111:4
- Psalm 112:4
- Psalm 116:5
- Psalm 145:8
- Joel 2:13
- Jonah 4:2

Hearing this once would be comforting, twice would be greatly reassuring, three times would be astounding. But ten times? Ten times we are told this is who God really is.

God wants us to get the point. Why? Because when we do not accept His nature, we will inevitably attribute the traumatic work of Satan as being the work of God. We will take the rejection coming at us from men, operating as unwitting agents of Satan, and assume it is the intent and will of God in Heaven. But God declares that darkness and light cannot mix.

> God is light, and **in him is no darkness at all**.
>
> 1 John 1:5

Now take heart, for God does not lie, and there is no variation in who He is.

> ...with whom there is **no variation or shadow of turning.**
>
> James 1:17

God does not lie, but man does!

> Let God be true but every man a liar
>
> Rom 3:4, NKJV

And most assuredly, the god of this present age lies:

> Whenever he tells a lie, he speaks from his own nature, because he is a liar and the **father of lies**.
>
> John 8:44, NASB

We need to get that monkey off our back! We need to break any agreement with the demonic tormentor that tells us rejection on Earth is Heaven's rejection of us as well. *Begone in Jesus' Name!*

We should have rock solid assurance as to who our God is and who He is not, so that when we are faced with persecution, rejection, or violation of any kind, we know whose side Heaven is on. Then we can approach the throne of mercy and grace in boldness and pray!

God sent His own Son so that we would experience *the opposite* of what the ruthless god of rejection had in store for us. Jesus showed us the will of His Father, who wants to fellowship with us, no matter how badly we have been abused or mistreated or rejected by the world. Jesus on the Cross became the open door of acceptance for us into the family of Heaven.

> "Most assuredly, I say to you, I am the door of the sheep."
>
> Jesus, John 10:7, NKJV

Jesus went so far as to accept a thief hanging on a cross next to him, inviting him into Heaven that same day, in the middle of his own traumatic death.

THE NATURE OF GOD
CONFIRMED FOR US IN THE NEW TESTAMENT

Did you notice that this definition of God was from an Old Testament source? It was *before* the work of Jesus in the New Testament. And, it had to be so!

Why?

Because Jesus came as the representation of the Father.

> [Jesus] is the radiance of His glory and the **exact representation of His nature**...
>
> Heb 1:3 NASB

If you know heart of the Son, you know the heart of the Father. If they had known the heart of the Father, they would not have rejected His Son. There is total unity in the majestic reign that comes down from the throne of Heaven.

> I and the Father are one.   Jesus, John 10:30

We find that truth about the nature of God which began in the Old Testament continues into the New Testament, unchanged, but where it shines even clearer and brighter. :

THE JESUS OF 1 CORINTHIANS 13

Consider the following from 1 John 4:

God is love   1 John 4:8 NKJV

God is love. And as we have just read, Jesus is the "exact representation" of His Father:

[Jesus] is the radiance of His glory and the **exact representation of His nature**...

Heb 1:3 NASB

Since *God is love* and *Jesus is the perfect representation of God*, we can conclude "*Jesus is also love.*"

With that established in our mind, let's review what First Corinthians has to say about love. When reading this passage on love, it is really describing Jesus, who is very definition of love and the exact representation of His Father.

"Love is patient, love is kind" - Jesus is patient, Jesus is kind.

"Love is not jealous; love does not brag, it is not arrogant." - Jesus is not jealous, does not brag and is not arrogant (or prideful). He speaks of Himself in Matthew 11 as humble; can you imagine?

Come to Me, all who are weary and burdened, and I will give you rest. Take My yoke upon you and learn from Me, **for I am gentle and humble in heart**, and you will find rest for your souls.

Matt 11:28–29 NASB

"Love does not act disgracefully, it does not seek its own benefit" - Jesus does not act disgracefully toward us (He is not ruthless or arrogant as the men in Psalm 86). He is not selfish because He does not seek His own benefit. His willingness to go to the Cross on our behalf is a roar from Heaven in our ears that is meant to overpower the shout of the enemy's lies. Even to this day, *He does not seek His own benefit, He is not self-centered; He always seeks our benefit instead!*

"**Love is not provoked**" - Jesus is not subject to outbursts of wrath, He is not angered by us or our mistakes. He is not "violent" like the men who opposed King David. He is instead like His Father, "gracious and compassionate" and "full of mercy and loving-kindness." He is especially this way toward those who run to Him for refuge. *You are the apple of His eye.*

"**Love does not keep an account of a wrong suffered**" - Jesus does not keep a record of the wrongs He has suffered by our indifference or our faithlessness toward Him. He is faithful to us even when we are not faithful to Him...

> If we are faithless, He remains faithful; He cannot deny Himself.
> 2 Tim 2:13

"**Love does not rejoice in unrighteousness, but rejoices with the truth**" - Jesus does not participate in the unrighteous acts of others, including those who reject us, aggressively oppose us, ruthlessly attack us or seek to incapacitate us through trauma.

"**Love keeps every confidence, it believes all things, hopes all things, endures all things.**" - Jesus believes in us! He is the gift of Hope to us. He watches us from His throne and cheers for us. He endures things alongside us, including the periods of trauma through which we at times walk.

"**Love never fails**" - Jesus will never fail us. He will never leave us; He will never forsake; He will never abandon us. The world will scream otherwise, because the god of this world is a liar.

> For He Himself has said, "**I will never leave you nor forsake you.**"
> Heb 13:5

Can you see how effectively the enemy has planted lies inside our head? The lies of the enemy are always the opposite of the truth of Heaven. Satan lies, but the truth of Jesus roars like the Lion of Judah back at him.

Who are we going to listen to? The Son of God who sits on Heaven's throne, or the deceiver who is destined to be bound in chains in hell?

> I saw an angel coming down from heaven, holding the key of the abyss and a great chain in his hand. And he took hold of the dragon, the serpent of old, **who is the devil and Satan,** and bound him... he threw him into the abyss and shut it and sealed it over him, **so that he would not deceive the nations any longer**
>
> Rev 20:1

The love of Jesus stands guard over us, even when we do not sense His presence or see His hand at work in the midst of our traumatic experience. Even when we are numb inside, Heaven is roaring with love toward us and will not stop until we, like Daniel's friends, emerge without ropes, without chains, and without even the smell of smoke on us.

6

SEXUAL TRAUMA: PURITY RESTORED

In Jesus we have love and acceptance.

Satan's ways are counterfeit to that of Heaven. In the last chapter we saw how Satan offers the opposite to acceptance; the opposite of acceptance is *rejection*. In this chapter, we will see how Satan also offers the opposite to Heaven's love. The opposite of love that originates in Heaven is called *lust*.

Many people have reached out to us for ministry who are dealing with *trauma from sex*. What God intended for good Satan has distorted and weaponized. We have seen many who suffered trauma from *the loss of innocence* at a young age, with an accompanying *fear of punishment* associated with the related spirits of *guilt* and *shame*. This chapter and the next share some of their stories.

Just as rejection can be a traumatic experience for us, so also lust can open doors to trauma in our lives, often by the actions others against us. The devil knows that...

The root of lust is rejection.

Through lust, a person uses or abuses another person without any concern for the sense of self worth, health or security of the other. That is a harsh form of rejection indeed.

Lust is an example of how prevalent the existence of evil spirits are in our world today. A person engaged in lust is self-oriented, in a compulsive way, and pursues self-gratification. This is the opposite of the sacrificial love that came down from Heaven, a love that came to serve others. Self-gratification seeks its own gain at the expense (or in the worst cases, the harm) of another.

A person driven by compulsive sexual obsessions is in dire need of deliverance from the *spirit of lust*, as well as other spirits that come along with it.[8] In many cases, sexual abuse in the early years a life opens the victim up to the nesting of sexual spirits like lust. The trauma of a sexual encounter, especially forced on a child, can crack that mirror of their personality described in Chapter 1. The love of Jesus comes with the power necessary to reverse its effect.

Heaven's love is the opposite of Satan's lust. God is love and His Son, Jesus, is love. True love does not disrespect, does not violate the will of another, causes no harm, and does not seek its own gratification (1 Cor 13). The love of Jesus counters the selfishness of lust offered by Satan. His love, *true love*, never fails.

TESTIMONY:
SEXUAL BROKENNESS

We lead those who come for ministry in a prayer, to commit or re-commit their lives to Jesus. We apply the blood of Jesus Christ to their body, mind and soul. Then, we then bind Satan and his dark powers at work through unclean, evil spirits. We use the authority given to Adam and then reinstated by Jesus to bind the enemy and then loose the captives (to set them free!).

After an initial dedication prayer to Jesus, we began to ask about a person's past, seeking the gifts of the Holy Spirit to guide us in what is taking place. As described earlier in Chapter 2, we ask a standard question at the outset: "try to recall your earliest recollections in life for us." This question, as mentioned, tends to reveal early trauma in the lives of those we are counseling without forcing the question.

In one case, a woman who ran weekly prayer meetings in her home asked us to counsel a young woman. The woman needing

---

8 Refer to the booklet, *Repercussions from Sexual Sins* by Frank Hammond for a list of unclean spirits that come with lust. Also for married couples, refer to the booklet *The Marriage Bed*, also by Frank Hammond. See the back of the book for more information.

ministry was in her thirties at the time. As the session began, we learned that she was living in what the world calls an "alternative lifestyle." We will call her Elizabeth, or *Beth* for short.

We began with our standard question: "Beth, would you try to recall your earliest recollections in life for us?"

Beth's mind went to an incident when, as a small child, she agreed with a little boy to expose herself to him as he exposed himself to her. Her mother, made aware of this, scolded and shamed her for this. The Holy Spirit revealed to that this was the moment when the *spirits of rejection* and *trauma* entered into her and altered the course of her life.

Beth's mother's intent was to stop Beth from doing things that would be harmful to her little soul. She intended to keep her little girl from being defiled. But in the heat of the moment, Beth's impression of her mother's disciplinary action was so shocking that it became a self-imposed perception that it was wrong for her to have sexual relations with a male, ever. While the intention of the mother was good, the shock and fear of punishment was traumatic to her little soul. In her case, it had the effect of steering her away from men altogether.

Over time, she developed into a youth with an active imagination, a healthy thing except that in her case, the enemy turned that toward sexual fantasy. When lust came knocking on her door, the trauma and fear of punishment about men was present, so Beth's mind wandered into fantasy about other women. At age eighteen she entered into her first sexual relationship. She had affairs with several women after that, with one affair lasting for many years.

The enemy told her this was all set in stone. He had convinced her that she was born a lesbian and could not change that fact. We, however, knew that her choices in life were not written in stone, and that the enemy is a liar. Beth was not born a lesbian, but she was a victim of trauma in her early years.

Her deliverance involved breaking the grip of the *spirit of trauma* that held her, as well as deliverance from the *confusion* and *lust* that originated from it.

Today, Beth is a confident woman, filled with the Spirit of the Lord and very active in a local Full Gospel Fellowship. When Satan says something is written in stone, Jesus is ready to counter him every time. When we seek Heaven's answer on a matter, Jesus is faithful to lead us into His truth and to show us that the enemy is both a liar and a thief. The truth was that Jesus loved Beth so much that He went to the cross on her behalf.

We all walk in the light we have; Beth's mother would never have knowingly scolded her child to the point of damaging her little soul. As any parent quickly learns, parenting in this overly sexualized world is difficult. The best medicine for little souls under their care is proactiveness. We remain proactive by seeking the guidance and counsel of the Holy Spirit. Parents should pray. They should apply the Blood of Jesus over the little hearts, minds and physical bodies of their children. This can start as early as the womb. Parents should remove any exposure to sex at a young age, but also be prepared to counter its effect when it sneaks in.

Parents should also observe their child's actions. If they sense sexuality encroaching on a young child, they should bind Satan's attempts at incursion. They should encourage children to pray openly, and they should listen to what their children are praying.

Our prayer for parents is that they would draw strength from the ministry of the Holy Spirit in this area, to keep both them and their little children on high, safe ground, undefiled by the encroachment of lust brought by the *god of this present age*:

He makes my feet like deer's feet, and **sets me up on my high places**.

Ps 18:33, NASB

Children grow into adults and adults define righteousness for society and the world. It should therefore come as no surprise that children are targets for harassment by the enemy.[9]

Little ones are the closest thing we have to the image of purity in Heaven. Their innocence is likened to the state of Adam and Eve in the Garden before temptation and sin entered. For us adults, the deliverance ministry of Jesus seeks to restore that child-like purity to us even though we have acquired emotional scars dealing with our own battles with sin. While we are meant to mature, we are also meant to seek righteousness and those things that are pure and holy. This is how we maintain a healthy state in an unstable and sexually traumatized world.

When His disciples were trying to chase away the children who were naturally drawn to Jesus, the Lord said:

"Leave the children alone, and do not forbid them to come to Me; **for the kingdom of heaven belongs to such as these.**"

Matt 19:14 NASB

There is a purpose in purity. God intends to use our purity as a weapon against Satan, while at the same time prepare a mature bride for His Son, Jesus.

THE FATHER PREPARES HIMSELF A BRIDE

Because of what Jesus went through on our behalf, He has received glory above all the hosts of Heaven. He has proven, in front of all powers and principalities looking on, that He is worthy.

---

9 For ministry to children refer to *Deliverance for Children & Teens* by Bill & Sue Banks, and *A Manual for Children's Deliverance* by Frank & Ida Mae Hammond. See the back of the book for more information.

> Then I looked, and I heard the voices of many angels around the throne and the living creatures and the elders...
>
> **"Worthy is the Lamb ... to receive power, wealth, wisdom, might, honor, glory, and blessing."**
> Rev 5:11–12, NASB

Jesus is most worthy, but worthy of what? He is worthy of honor and glory for sure. He is worthy of the kind of power that comes with the full authority of God in Heaven, where He also sits on a throne:

> ... seek those things which are above, **where Christ is, sitting at the right hand of God**.
> Col 3:1

The Father is quite proud of His Son, as He should be. The only sure way to honor God the Father is by showing respect and love to His Son. Jesus declared this when He told us, "no one comes to the Father except through Me" (John 14:6).

> **We receive acceptance by the Father by our acceptance of His Son. We receive blessing from the Father when show thankfulness for the accomplishments of His Son.**

By staying the course through to the Cross, and conquering death as a resurrected, fully alive Savior (Deliverer) of mankind, Jesus become worthy to receive many things. The kingly crown and the throne are perhaps the most famous gifts the Father bestowed on the Son.

But there was something else in the heart of the Father that He had in mind for His Son. This gift was special and touched the heart of the Father deeply. The Father intends to honor His Son with a soul mate, a bride that is beautiful, strong and wise. This princess is going to reign on the Throne alongside His Son, the Prince of Peace.

The process of us becoming clean, much like Esther in the court of Persia, is intended to make ourselves ready to serve the King in this supporting role.

> Let us be glad and rejoice, and give honour to him: for the marriage of the Lamb is come, and **his wife hath made herself ready**.
>
> Rev 19:7, NKJV

There is a reason why we are called the Bride of Christ:

> **The reason we are referred to as a** Bride in waiting **is because God wants to emphasize the need for purity in our lives.**

Whether we know it or not, we are being prepared for our upcoming role to share in the administration of His kingdom. What kind of Bride does Jesus intend to come back for?

> Christ also loved the church and **gave Himself up for her** [His Bride], so that He might sanctify her, having cleansed her by the washing of water with the word, that He might present to Himself the church in all her glory, **having no spot or wrinkle or any such thing; but that she would be holy and blameless.**
>
> Eph 5:25–27 [Parenthesis Mine], NKJV

We are that Bride without "spot or wrinkle," who is "holy and blameless." In other words, Jesus is coming back to claim a people who have chosen purity over the lusts of the world. We are called to *set ourselves apart* and to break with the sin patterns of the world. While we cannot erase the stain of our past, Jesus can. Our Redeemer has made a way where there was no way for us to be made clean.

> **The Cross provides a continual fountain of cleansing for us, His Bride. The reading of His Word also provides a continual fountain of cleansing for us.**

Water baptism is a powerful, visual example of how we are cleansed from our past and thus receive a new life set apart for Him. Our sins are "washed away" as we emerge from the waters of baptism.

Baptism by water points to the ongoing process of cleansing that will follow us as we move forward and grow into maturity. After all, *who doesn't need a bath every once in a while?*

Heaven is opening the taps of living water in order to shower righteousness upon us, to cleanse us.

> I will sprinkle clean water on you, and you will be clean; I will cleanse you from all your filthiness and from all your idols.
> Ez 36:25, NASB

I tell those who come for ministry that deliverance is precisely that: walking into a shower of righteous light coming down from Heaven's throne, and we are cleansed from demonic defilement and made whole. It is encouraging to know that, as we step into Heaven's shower of righteousness, that we emerge not naked and shivering, but clothed in a warm, white robe or righteousness as we walk with Jesus:

> ... they will **walk with Me in white**, for they are worthy.
> Rev 3:4, NASB

This is a special message of the Lord to those who have been subjected to sexual abuse. He is coming back for you, and will claim you as spotless, without wrinkle, and cleansed completely from your trauma. He is wanting to robe you in a blindingly white robe of righteousness. I would say that is something to get excited about.

> I will rejoice greatly in the Lord, my soul will be joyful in my God; for He has clothed me with garments of salvation, **He has wrapped me with a robe of righteousness**... **as a bride** adorns herself with her jewels.
> Is 61:10, NASB

The contrast could not be more stark. While Satan and his agents are robed in a cloak of darkness, we are clothed in a white robe of light. This is very clear to the spiritual forces looking on in supernatural realm.

If we sin, and the enemy tosses a bucket of mud on our beautiful white robe, we turn to the Lord through repentance, and we step right back into the shower. The taps in Heaven are open to wash us again, and again. Our robe is restored to its pristine, white original state, just as it was before and without any spot of mud or stain.

An honest person would tell you that mud gets tossed on each of us, often. Jesus went to the Cross knowing this. He made provision for us to be cleansed over and over again as we mature in our role as the bride in waiting. As we walk out the process of maturing, and are loosed from the compulsive nature of evil spirits, the shower may be needed less and less, but it is still there ready when we need it. King David certainly needed it, even later in life, as do we:

> **Wash me throughly** from mine iniquity, and **cleanse me from my sin**... Purge me with hyssop, **and I shall be clean**: wash me, and **I shall be whiter than snow**.
>
> Ps 51:2, 7

Evil spirits are by nature "unclean," so the driving out of unclean spirits is related to the process of us being cleansed and prepared to be a bride without spot or blemish. Deliverance from evil spirits, including spirits of *trauma, abuse, lust, hatred, fear, guilt, shame* and such, is a form of being washed and cleansed. It is a cleansing process separate from salvation, because nothing can separate us from the love of Jesus (even demons).

> For I am convinced that **neither death, nor life, nor angels, nor principalities** [*demons*], nor things present, nor things to come, nor powers, nor height, nor depth, nor any other created thing **will be able to separate us from the love of God that is in Christ Jesus our Lord.**
>
> Rom 8:38–39, NASB [Brackets Mine]

Rather, deliverance is related to our maturity to reign with Jesus in the ages to come.

THE TABLE IS BEING SET AND
THE INVITATIONS HAVE BEEN SENT OUT

You, my dear friend, are that beautiful bride robed in white, in waiting. You have been invited to the feast to come to celebrate, "the marriage supper of the Lamb." Forget the past, leave it behind. Prepare yourself to meet the One who redeemed you through His love for you:

> Let us be glad and rejoice, and give honour to him: for the **marriage of the Lamb** is come, and his wife hath made herself ready. And to her was granted that she should be arrayed in fine linen, clean and white: for the fine linen is the righteousness of saints... Blessed are they which are called unto **the marriage supper of the Lamb**.
>
> Rev 19:7–9

Jesus, now seated on His throne, is preparing all of Heaven for a great feast so that when He comes back to claim this woman of purity, He can introduce her in person to the rest of the Heaven's family. The table is being set and the invitations have been sent out. Your name is on the list!

Jesus invites all to come to the feast regardless of our past, and how traumatic its effect has been on our heart and mind. Now is the time to accept His invitation to this feast, for a time is coming when the door to the marriage feast will be shut. For this reason, Jesus warns us all to be alert, sober minded, and to watch:

> **Watch therefore**, for ye know neither the day nor the hour wherein the Son of man cometh.
>
> Matt 25:13

PURITY OPENS THE DOOR TO HOLINESS

As the people of God, the Bride of Christ, we are called to be set apart as a "holy nation."

HOLINESS VITAL TO COPING 83

> But you are a chosen people, a royal priesthood, **a holy nation**,
> a people for God's own possession...
>
> 1 Peter 2: 9, NASB

How do we become holy?

As we hunger and thirst for righteousness (of which purity belongs), we enter into His presence, As we enter His presence, holiness shows up and we are made holy. It is *His holiness* that comes upon us, not our own. Our conscience decision to pursue righteousness (and purity) opens the door to His presence and that is what makes us holy.

> **Our part is to seek purity and righteousness, His part is to bestow on us holiness.**

God knows that purity leading to holiness is not easily attained, especially in our sexually-obsessed, sexually-charged world. So He sent us a *helper!* The Holy Spirit, the strong Spirit of the Lord, is here to prepare the Bride for the soon return of the Son:

> Not by might, nor by power, **but by my spirit**, saith the Lord of hosts.
>
> Zech 4:6, KJV

The Spirit's work is to prepare us this process is called "sanctification." To sanctify means, simply, *to be made holy*. As He is holy, so must His people be as well:

> Therefore **gird up the loins of your mind**, be sober, and rest your hope fully upon the grace that is to be brought to you at the revelation of Jesus Christ; as obedient children, not conforming yourselves to the former lusts, as in your ignorance; but as He who called you is holy, you also be holy in all your conduct, because it is written, "**Be holy, for I am holy.**"
>
> 1 Peter 1:13–16

When believers in Jesus are coming out of a past of sexual abuse, the Lord is very capable and willing to remove all spot and stain, to make us new creations in Heaven's sight. He promises to make us as *white as snow:*

> Therefore if anyone is in Christ, **this person is a new creation**; the old things passed away; behold, new things have come.
>
> 2 Cor 5:17

Let me give you a few examples of His ministry to victims of abuse to show you there is no wall too high or mountain too big for our God to conquer.

RAPE, A TRAUMA FROM SATAN

We were asked to see a young woman in her thirties several years ago. When prompted to recall early events in her life, she said she remembered nothing before age 21. The one event she could recall was rape. I'm sure there was much of her youth and childhood she could have remembered, but the Holy Spirit was in charge. Time was short and He brought the incident to her mind.

The trauma of this terrifying abuse to her body opened the way for the spirits of fear and insecurity. Afraid she would become promiscuous, she soon married. However, this brought more trauma. The traumatic memories, coupled with the pressure brought by unclean spirits, prevented her from entering into normal relations with her husband. He then beat her and raped her until she finally divorced him.

The next husband was a pastor who had problems of his own. He had unclean spirits of *pornography* and *fantasy lust.* This marriage went the same way. Eventually she divorced him.

The third marriage lasted only a few weeks. She left after the first beating.

This is about the time we entered her life and began to minister to her. We had to deal with the *spirit of trauma* from rape and violence that came against her from men. She was set on a beautiful path of recovery, so free that she was able to envision herself in a marriage again but with a true man of God. That was how we knew she was free from the trauma of her past.

Today, she is completely healed. But she needs reassurance in certain areas when the liar shows up and begins to speak in her ear. People who experience these types of traumas need more than deliverance, they need healing as well. Jesus came to "heal the broken-hearted." Even after the healing, they need continued counseling, prayer, advice and support. This lady has called us from several states away on numerous occasions. She is still sending in good reports. Praise the Lord!

TESTIMONY:
SEXUAL TRAUMA BY A VOODOO PRIEST

A lady once called for prayer. She was living in the United States, but had grown up in an poor country where people were largely under the influence of witch doctors (*juju* or *voodoo* priests). Her parents, ignorant to the enemy's devices and intending to be good, religious people, tried to cover their bases. They took her to church on Sunday mornings and then the voodoo priest on Sunday afternoons.

Putting a young child in that environment was tragic. Over the course of multiple sessions, the voodoo priest began to rape her as part of his "cleansing ritual." The powers of Satan are always directed towards the harming of children, whether it is in a rich nation or a poor one.

Through the trauma of repeated rapes, the spirit of trauma and other unclean spirits entered that young girl as she was taken to these rituals. Her life took on tragic overtones as she grew and eventually left home. In years that followed, she fell prey to many sexual predators and eventually settled into one of the most promiscuous lifestyles imaginable, with multiple partners in multiple settings and multiple partners in a single setting, of both sexes. The devil was taking his fury out on her.

God did not abandon her, though. He does not abandon his kids.

When she finally met the Lord and gave her life to Jesus, she became a *new creation*. She fell in love with Jesus because she encountered the reality of Heaven. She settled down, married a good Christian man and was about to start a family. That is why she called.

She had a persistent problem. The demonic spirit from the voodoo priest would visit her some nights and continue to rape her while she tried to sleep; even into adulthood. This may sound outlandish to our scientific, rational minds, but spiritual attacks of this nature are on the rise because of the rampant abuse of children in today's world. We have encountered many men and women who have lived in the shadows because of what happens to them at night and the shame and fear of telling others that results.

There was nothing we could do in the natural for this tormented soul. Words would never be enough. But as Daniel told the King in Babylon, "There is a God in Heaven who can!" Even though she was a thousand miles away and speaking by phone, that did not stop the work of the Holy Spirit from coming into the room strong on her behalf.

As we began to pray, we called down the armies of Jesus in Heaven to go to war against the spirit of rape prowling in this woman's life. We bound the evil spirit from the priest from operating any further; we bound it according to the teaching of Jesus in Matthew 12. By faith, we locked him up in chains, and we stripped him of his power and influence on her life. We commanded the spiritual forces looking on to pay attention and to flee. And then we asked for the cleansing work of the Holy Spirit to pour over her like a shower the Throne of Jesus in Heaven. I pictured this woman, on the other end of the phone, stepping into a spiritual shower of light, her life being cleansed completely from the trauma and torment of this spirit of rape, and his unclean companions.

What happened next matched the level of warfare this woman was under. As soon as those simple words had been spoken, the Holy Spirit took over and filled the room from where she was calling. HE went on the attack, and broke that perverted spirit of rape. Our friend screamed loudly, hit the floor, and began to roll around as the spirit screamed its way out of her.

Jesus reclaimed His Bride that day.

In her words after the fact, she told is how she began to shake angrily from within herself, kicking and screaming under this spirit's rage on the floor until it had left. After about 10 minutes of this protest the spirit left. She spent the next 20 minutes laughing and crying out loud in joy to the Lord, still on the floor. Far, far greater is the Holy Spirit within us than the defiling, demonic powers who attempt to resist eviction. When she finally able to sit up, she knew she was completely free. Where there had been fear and trauma there was now an incredible peace and calm. There were many shouts of joy on her side of the phone, and on our side as well!

The strong arm of the Lord had done all the work; we did not even have her full name and were doing our best to pray over the phone from a thousand miles away! Yes, this was 100% in the hands of the Lord and the Spirit of the Lord gets all the glory.

A few months later she called to confirm that she had no harassment after that day, and was still bubbling inside from the freedom she tasted from the absence of trauma and torment. And, to make matters even better, she was now expecting her first child.

UNCLEAN SPIRITS THAT HARASS AT NIGHT

People who struggle with sexual visitations at night are trapped in two traumas at once: first there is the darkness and the defilement that surrounds them in the night, and then there is the trauma of the fear of others finding out. How does one ask for prayer against such an attack without being ostracized or labeled mentally ill?

It is time for the Church to grow up and step up.

Can you imagine how displeased Jesus will be to learn that we ran away from people suffering the effects of trauma, especially when it is attacking them in their own beds?

As occult involvement by the general population spreads, including Eastern mysticism, so the sexual defilement associated with it spreads, and with consequences. The blood of Jesus overpowers the hold an unclean sexual spirit has on His children, and the Spirit comes with the knockout punch to purge defilement out of the Bride. The Spirit of the Lord drives out, or casts out, the spirit and even severs any soul tie to a person in the past.[10]

> But **if I cast out demons** with the finger of God, **surely the kingdom of God has come upon you**.
>
> Jesus Speaking, Luke 11:20

Deliverance ministers have shared countless stories of people being attacked in similar sexual manner at night. For example, Frank Hammond tells a story of ministering to a Jamaican man who, along with relatives, had been deeply involved in voodoo. He was being tormented nightly by a *sexual* spirit of rape. Not knowing the ways of God, in his desperation for help he had sought the help of a witch.

After going through a witchcraft ritual, the problem was even worse than before. Now this man required deliverance from both witchcraft spirits he acquired from the "cleansing ritual" and the

10 Refer to the booklet *Soul Ties* by Frank Hammond, and *Breaking Unhealthy Soul Ties* by Bill & Sue Banks. See the back of the book for more information.

original spirit that would attack him sexually at night.

It is understandable that people are often embarrassed to admit that they are having night visitations from sexual spirits, but it is the devil who makes people feel ashamed and afraid. We must expose the devil by bringing secret things into the light.[11] That is what he fears the most. Light shining on darkness is the greatest antiseptic for the soul. When light shines on dark places, the darkness has to flee.

11 Compiled from *Confronting Familiar Spirits*, by Frank Hammond, available as a book or e-book. Also as an Audio teaching entitled: *Triumphing Over Familiar Spirits (CD)*. See the back of the book for more information.

7

THE TRAUMA OF INCEST:
NO PROBLEM IS TOO BIG FOR OUR GOD

Incest is a nesting place for Satan. The eighteenth chapter of Leviticus forbids sexual relations with close relatives, including parents with children and children with parents. The nineteenth chapter of Genesis delivers a graphic example of how the trauma from incest can create oppressive effects that torment victims for generations to come, without the intervention of the delivering power of Jesus Christ.

After God rescued Lot and his daughters from Sodom, with the loss of his wife as a pillar of salt, Lot took up residence in a cave with his two daughters. Without any men to marry, his daughters schemed to get him drunk on wine and then had sexual relations with him as he slept. There were no other men around, and with the destruction they had just witnessed, they reasoned this was the only way to continue the family line (Genesis 19:32). In the aftermath of seeing their homeland destroyed by fire from above, and the traumatic footprint it stamped on their minds, they left out God's ability to provide husbands and to bless them with children in the years to come. Their traumatic experience and the despair it left on them led to incest.

But trauma from the destruction they witnessed in Sodom was only part of their problem; there was trauma from before that as well. This trauma arose from their father and mother.

Their father, Lot, consistently chose the natural over the spiritual (Genesis 13:10-11). Because of this, he was ensnared by the enemy who was deeply associated with Sodomites (Genesis 14:12). The population of Sodom had surrendered to ruthless evil and Lot was attempting to live amongst it without shining too bright a light.

Lot was faced with pressures living in such a godless society, and was weakened as a result in his witness. He was even unable to convince the men pledged to marry his daughters of their impending doom (Genesis 19:14); his life up to that point did not carry a testimony into the lives of these young men. Hence when he came with the news, they shrugged and laughed.

Lot was also a procrastinator, arguing with the Lord when told to flee immediately from his home (Genesis 19:18-21). He had a disobedient wife who had become ensnared herself with the wealth and possessions they had in Sodom (Genesis 19:26).

Trauma can bring about many reactions. Lot stood at the door of his house with two strangers taken into his home (the angels sent to rescue him). The men of Sodom outside were threatening to break the door down and take the men under his protection to be used for their sexual pleasures. There was a spirit of rape breathing hot breath on his door. Lot reacted to the pressure by offering his virgin daughters to the men outside in return for the visitors' safety. That must have left those poor girls *traumatized!*

These same girls had to then watch as their mother rebelled against the instruction of the angels, causing her to turn into a pillar of salt, dead before their eyes. Now, they had lost their city, their mother, their friends, most of the respect for their father who was their protector, and their future husbands.

The bottom line is that it seems from the Biblical account that both parents of these young girls were living after the flesh, a bad setup for what was about to come. How important is this lesson for us today? Jesus refers to their weakened state when he speaks of the days we are in now, leading up to His return:

> "Remember Lot's wife!"
>
> Jesus Speaking of the last days, Luke 17:32 KJV

To paraphrase, *"learn from their lesson!"*

It is not too great a stretch to consider his daughters were not counseled well by their father to resist panic and fear. They were unprepared for the confrontation that was to come between the righteousness of Heaven and the wickedness of Sodom. They were also alone, emotionally, to face the trauma that came with the destruction of their home and their city and all the people they knew.

Trauma can have so great an impact on a person's mind and emotions that a pattern of bizarre behavior begins to emerge. A person can become frozen in place and cease to function in rational ways. Had the daughters of Lot sought the Lord for their future, they would have been rewarded by God, according to His timing. Consider that their uncle, Abraham, had to wait to be 100 years old before he saw the fulfillment of the Lord's prophecy; that we would be the father to many nations.

> Then Abraham fell on his face and laughed, and said in his heart, "Shall a child be born to a man who is one hundred years old? And shall Sarah, who is ninety years old, bear a child?"
>
> Gen 17:17

Nevertheless, their uncle Abraham knew that His God was a promise keeper, faithful in all His ways; that God is always able to make a way where there is no way, as a problem-solving, solutions-oriented God.

TESTIMONY:
THE INCEST, RAPE, ABUSE AND *TRIUMPH* OF JANET[12]

A woman whom we will call Janet was referred to us for ministry. We discovered early in our initial counseling session that she suffered from controlling and tormenting demonic voices, as well as actual physical abuse from demonic forces. She had been married four times and had an eleven year old son from still another relationship. She lived in public, low-income housing and was in a rehabilitation program, which provided secular counseling and employment.

Janet's problems began early on in her life. She had been sexually molested as a small child by uncles, her brothers and even her mother. Her father abused her physically. She suffered from verbal abuse and abandonment most of her life. All that trauma and abuse led to a nest of spiritual problem, far too great for society to solve but never too great for Jesus Christ.

So great was the attack on her life we witnessed spiritual manifestations firsthand. We actually observed invisible forces beating her on her arms, body and neck as we spoke to her. *Bruise marks appeared on her skin from these spirit attacks, as we watched.*

This was all happening in our first ministry session with Janet. We had a strong anointing of the Lord on the room that day; her Deliverer Jesus was present!

We taught her how her senses were the entrance ways to her inner self. We explained to her how the blood on the doorpost in Egypt protected the Israelites at the time of the exodus. We then translated that point to her own body. By laying her own hand on herself, she sealed her doors against continued intrusion by destructive spirits. By symbolically applying the Blood of Jesus, abuse was greatly

---

12 Compiled from the book *Deliverance for Children & Teens* by Bill & Sue Banks. See the back of the book for more information.

curtailed. Her will was engaged; she even took a broom and began to symbolically sweep the forces of evil out the door of her apartment, loudly commanding them to leave her residence as well. She did this in the Name of Jesus. Immediately thereafter she said she saw dark clouds leaving her body by way of her mouth.

After several sessions, the demonic beatings and bruising stopped. However, the voices remained. She asked questions such as, "Will the Holy Spirit tell me to do bad things? Will the devil ever tell me to do good things?" She was troubled by religious spirits and spirits of guilt. The religious people in her life had her greatly confused about what is right and what is wrong in the eyes of God.

As I was explaining to her that the Holy Spirit will never lead us into evil, I felt impressed there was something dark in her past that she was hiding. I said, "The devil dwells in darkness and secrecy because he fears exposure to the light and to the truth. Tell us what you are still holding on to."

She then confessed guilt concerning her mother's violent death. I pressed for the circumstances. Although she was just a witness to her mother's death, as a child she blamed herself, and she retained guilt over it ever since. I then managed to convince her that she should let all of her feelings of guilt go, to "cast it all on Jesus who cares for her." She sensed an immediate release in her spirit.

In our next session, she told me how free she felt from the demons that traumatized her for so long, but she still retained a "dead feeling" inside of herself. I made the point that the emptiness from all those trespassers leaving her soul needed to be filled with the good things of the Kingdom of Heaven, like peace and joy, and this comes only through the Holy Spirit. She left the session that day pondering how God could bring joy back to her life given the dire emptiness of her soul.

Within minutes the phone rang again. It was Janet! She felt alive and full. She excitedly proclaimed that she was singing and praising to the Lord, and as she forced herself to begin the Lord broke through. She said that she had not been that happy nor had she praised the Lord like that for a great number of years.

Janet, the product of incest, rape and abuse as a child, was now free of the torment and torture that had held her in bondage for most of her entire life. Thankfully, a part of her never gave in. A part of her never quit holding out for survival, and God honored her desire and her perseverance.

Today Janet knows she must continue to stand her ground, and when necessary, to fight her battle. Step by step she is learning to put those tormentors on the run. After a few weeks of effort, she was sensing a power over them that would only grow with each new day. A routine had to be established in her life of resistance and replacement. She had to resist the enemy and replace his thoughts with the promises of Jesus. Every morning and every night she had to sit down and read through a list of Scriptures confirming the goodness of the Lord. This is how she fought her battle.

Janet carries her Bible with her to work. She witnesses to her fellow workers and shares her testimony as she rejoices in the peace she says she has found through the expulsion of those demons who had tormented and beaten her for so many years. Jesus says that if you are set free, you are free indeed (John 8:36)! Nahum 1:9 says that affliction shall not rise again. The Word of God does not lie. Janet is free and happy in her new life in Christ Jesus. She knows she is a new creation and the old tortured self is not even remembered in Heaven.

People who converse with the devil are going to lose. He is a liar and a tormentor; he seeks to traumatize us with lies. He is too sly for the natural mind. When Janet first came to us, she was a prime example. It took weeks for us to get her to stop listening to demon voices and to praise the Lord instead. Next, she learned to begin ignoring them. Only then were we able to prepare and condition her to hear the voice of the Lord.

Incest is far too common in our society today. While society rejoiced over the sexual revolution of the 1960s, and the liberation they thought it would bring, people today are slow to realize how this liberation has spread like a virus to younger and younger ages. They are also slow to realize that opening the doors to sexual liberality eventually causes harm to children, for that is the devil's original goal through all his various forms of defilement: he goes after the kids.

A fellow deliverance minister, Bill Banks, shared the following account of how a spirit of incest can present even though the victim may not know what the word even means.

INCEST OPERATES UNDETECTED[13]

A group of about 30 young people in their late teens from a rural community about 80 miles south of our city had gone to a nearby state park one Halloween evening after a party and decided to "try deliverance" as they had seen it done in a movie.

They all stood in a circle on top of a hill in the park and someone suggested that they cast demons out of one another. No sooner did the game begin than it ended abruptly — for they were all knocked from their feet and sent tumbling head over heels down the hill. None were seriously hurt, only scrapes and bruises occurred in the natural, but most of them picked up spirits of fear of demons and

13 Compiled from the book *Power for Deliverance: The Songs of Deliverance*, by Bill Banks. See the back of the book for more information.

terror of the Devil, as well as other *spirits of fear*. A ministry in their town had managed to deal with most of the individuals, but they were unable to help one serious cases. They called us for help.

The young man came for ministry during a public meeting we were holding in our area. I led the boy in a prayer of repentance for playing with the devil, and then took authority over the spirits keeping him in bondage. The boy indicated that he did not have any sense what was holding him in its grip. So, I commanded the first spirit, the "strongman," to name itself.

With absolutely no change of expression and no emotion, the boy responded out loud, "*incest.*"

I was surprised at how quickly the demon responded. I was also surprised at how he had displayed no remorse or embarrassment when he named the spirit moments earlier.

I began to command it to leave but there was absolutely no response. A moment later the Lord dropped a thought in my mind: does this boy even know what the word *incest* means?

So I asked him, "Do you know what incest is?" He replied, "No, I've never heard that word before." In deference to the women present I walked over to him and gently leaned to whisper the definition into his ear, "Incest is having sexual relations with a member of your own family."

Just as I got the words out of my mouth and the understanding began to dawn on his face, it all broke loose. He let out a loud, *growling* groan and slipped out of the chair onto the floor. A prolonged battle ensued for two and a half hours.

He went through physical gyrations that were impossible in the natural: he bent into a rigid 45 degree angle shape with his forehead on the floor and his toes on the floor, his backside pointing at the ceiling. Then he bounced in that position for minutes!

A little later he rolled over and curled up into a "V" shape with his navel on the floor, head and feet pointing toward the ceiling and bounced up and down in that position! This went on for at least 15 minutes.

He writhed and rolled on the floor for about an hour more before he was finally delivered. He sat up at last, wringing with sweat, the church parlor smelling like a gym, but praise God this boy was free!

We could see it merely by the joy beaming from his face, a face which moments earlier had been distorted into a bestial grimace and snarl. Now, there was a light about him, the light of Heaven that had showered him in its righteousness and love. We made sure he was aware that Jesus had freed him from guilt, freed from shame, and freed from the defilement that Satan had brought into his life through a sexual predator within his own family.

INCEST TESTIMONY:
MULTIPLE PERSONALITIES

Only by rebirth, made available through the regenerating power of the shed blood of Jesus Christ, are the "ripples" of Satan's reign over us made to cease. When a pebble is thrown into a pond from the shore, there are three results. It strikes the water, it sinks beneath the surface, and the ripple or result proceeds from the point of contact out toward the shore.

So it is with a demonic attack. He strikes, he enters, and the ripples are the effects of his attack as they endure, sometimes for *generations to come*. This is true whether it comes from yielding to a traumatic encounter with sin, or from an actual traumatic experience no fault of our own.

Once, during a service we were conducting in a small southern town, a 10-year-old boy came forward from his pew leading his mother by the hand. Neither of them said anything, they just stood before us. I knelt down to the youngster's level and put my arms around him. I prayed for him momentarily and then I led him in a sinner's prayer. He responded with conviction and sincerity. Then his mother said that he had pulled her from her pew, saying he wanted my wife Eve to pray for him. So as my wife knelt down, and put her arms around him, she prayed for him as well. It was such a sweet moment for us, and a new life was added to the eternal Kingdom of Heaven.

Days later we received a letter from the mother with pictures of the boy. Enclosed was a letter written by the boy himself.

However, a short time later, we received an urgent call from the pastor of the church, who informed us that earlier that morning, the boy had flown into a rage, broken a window, destroyed some furniture and attacked his mother at their home. The pastor urged us to come and counsel with the mother.

This is a powerful example of the vital need for the ministry of deliverance, even after salvation. To the women with the child grievously vexed by a demon, Jesus in His wisdom told her that the casting out of demons is "the children's bread." Jesus meant it was for the children of the Kingdom and not for those outside the Kingdom (Mark 7).

Our Ministry Began with the Mother

We went that same day and met with the mother and the grandmother as well, in the pastor's office. As we probed for information on the source of these violent outbursts in the young boy, we came across an unexpected past in the mother.

The church knew the mother by a name we will call "Emily," but she had signed the letter sent to us as "Rachel" (actual names have been changed). We were surprised to hear that her name was Emily and not Rachel.

In asking about this, we discovered she had a *dual identity,* or what the world calls a *multiple personality.*

Through further discussion we learned that "Rachel" represented the good in her life, while "Emily" represented all the bad. This, as we suspected, stemmed from her childhood. Emily was the true name of the mother of the boy, and Emily had a terrible childhood.

Her natural father had left her mother when she was very young. Her mother soon married again, but the next husband raped his stepdaughter time and time again while her mother was at work. To keep Emily from telling her mother, the man would lock her in a dark closet in the basement for hours at a time as a threat.

Eventually, he abandoned the family, but he coerced Emily to go with him. He threatened in secret to kill this young girl and her mother if she refused to go. He took her to a city in a northern state, where Emily lived day to day in state of fear.

The Lord had His eye on Emily to rescue her. Soon she met a Christian woman who brought her into her home and encouraged her to go to church. In time, Emily was free from the control of this abusive father figure. She met a man, married and had a son, the boy who received Jesus at our meeting and was now in need of desperate ministry.

Here we see the ripple effect in action. The trauma Emily had experienced with her stepfather had opened the door for many spirits, including rejection, fear, guilt, shame, lust, promiscuity, hatred, rage, murder and suicide. This nest of spirits was all present in her life. Added to this list was self-rejection and escapism. This is how Emily coped with the trauma forced upon her, and how she came to adopt the name Rachel as her good side.

Emily's marriage was not well, either. Abuse so often begets more abuse. The man she married was abusive towards her. She had conceived the son while being raped by her new husband. The demonic defilement inside her had attracted more abuse and more trauma toward itself, like a magnet. Now she was married to a sexual abuser as well.

Praise the Lord, this son ten years later had led her by the hand to pray salvation with my wife and I at that service a few weeks earlier. This was possible because a pastor had remained faithful to shine a light for Jesus, a mother was able to find a legitimate house of God to hear the good news of Jesus, and the Holy Spirit was present and working on that little boy's heart. All those were part of the miracle of her story and the miracle God was about to do for her son.

God works things together for good.

A Spirit of Rage Ruled over the Mother, and now the Son

Terrible and violent abuse was perpetrated against Emily again and again, all against her conscious permission and desire. The trauma of being abused opened her soul to a *spirit of rage* against those around her. There were two sides of the demonic kingdom at work in her life: the weakness that drew sexual abuse to her, and then the rage that poured out of her as a result.

The act of conceiving a child, which normally should be a beautiful experience, was a terribly traumatic experience for Emily. So added to her anger and bitterness against her stepfather was the knowledge that her own beloved son had been conceived during an act of rape by her abusive husband.

The enemy took advantage of that traumatic beginning of life for that little boy, and now the son was manifesting the same *spirit of rage* that was present in his mother. This is what led to the demonic episode and the urgent call from the pastor, where the young lad broke a window, damaged furniture and physically attacked his mother in their home.

The spiritual realm does not always operate in a way that is understandable to our rationale minds. But in this particular case, the pieces were coming together in a clear and concise manner.

Demons certainly use trauma as a means of entrance; the evidence in this regard is overwhelming. Just as evident, however, are the results of the ripple effect demonic activity has on the person and their offspring. They intend to remain and continue manifesting into succeeding generations, until they are eventually cast out by the power of the Holy Spirit in the name of Jesus of Nazareth.

With the pieces of the puzzle in place, my wife Eve and I were able to address the issue of rage in the mother's life, and the trauma that had caused her personality to split at such a young age. We were also keen to address whatever spirit was lingering in the family that may be attracting sexual abuse. Cutting them both free from the chains caused by incest and rape was the only way we knew to bring Heaven to Earth in the midst of this traumatized but precious family. Jesus died knowing He would be releasing the power to end this cycle of sexual torment and abuse, and to quench the fires of rage that burned as a result. It was really His work, not ours, that brought this family peace in their home and peace in their soul. Jesus is good.

8
THE MIND AND THE WILL

I, Paul Fernandez, am a native of Miami. I grew up in the subtropics of South Florida. I was eighteen years old before I saw my first snow. I observed what it looked like from the deck of a ship while viewing the mountains along the coast of Portugal. That was my first experience with snow!

My wife, Eve, on the other hand was born in Northeast Mississippi. She was well used to snow.

The first time her parents came to visit us in Miami it was during winter. The first words out of her father's mouth were "*Paul everything here is so green!*" He was greatly impressed with the fact that the trees do not shed their leaves in the winter. Before the day was over, he remarked to my wife that he was finding our new home in Miami to be "like a paradise."

Now suppose for a moment that my first trip North had been during winter. Assume that I had never seen trees shed their leaves in the Fall. Now, for the first time, I am up North in winter and all I see are dead trees; I would believe that those trees were dead because they looked dead and not a green leaf was to be found.

Now the good folks up North try to assure me that these trees are not dead, that they will come back to life again come Spring. But I just can't believe it; I don't trust what they are telling me because my eyes are seeing an entirely different reality. How could dead trees be resurrected back to life?

This is the position so many people take regarding the circumstances in life, and the miracles, healings and deliverance from evil spirits they read about in Scripture. Those things are dead to them; they died a long time ago.

I know, however, and have had experiences with angelic protection and demonic manifestations. I know and have seen miracles and healings, and experienced utterances of knowledge and wisdom given by the Holy Spirit. Others can even tell you of an experience with death, of a visit to heaven or hell or of having seen Jesus Christ Himself. I knew a man in Chicago who was as mean as skunk up until his 80s, when Jesus walked into his room one night. After that, he was an entirely different man, one of the sweetest men I had ever known. Now how does someone go from being an abusive man to filled to overflowing with love for the people around him, overnight? He was a dead tree that came back to life, and it happened when he met Jesus face to face.

Are these people with testimonies of the miraculous lying? Or have they seen Spring, when the dead trees turn again to life, green leaves return to the trees, and flowers bloom in their glorious colors?

The point I am making is this; even if we have not yet personally seen the miraculous, God is still a miracle working God, and God chooses to substantiate His Word *with manifestations*. We know this because Jesus said so.

In Mark 16:17-18, Jesus lists the signs that will follow or accompany those who believe in Him:

> And these signs shall follow them that believe; **In my name shall they cast out devils** [*demons*]; they shall **speak with new tongues**; They shall take up serpents; and if they drink any deadly thing, it shall not hurt them; **they shall lay hands on the sick, and they shall recover.**
>
> Mark 16:17–18 KJV [Parenthesis Mine]

Believers are told by Jesus to cast out demons, speak in new tongues, have no fear of snakes (evil spirits), and lay hands on the sick that they might recover. All of this is to be done in the Name of Jesus, and not by human or fleshly means; these things happen through the power and the might of the Holy Spirit. There will be no boasting or bragging in the Kingdom to come because it was all the work of the Spirit of the Lord, anyway! As it is with salvation, so it is with the working of miracles; it is the Holy Spirit who gets the credit:

> For by grace are ye saved through faith; and that not of yourselves: it is the gift of God: **not of works, lest any man should boast**.
>
> Eph 2:8–9

THE BATTLE ABOVE WAGES
IN SUPPORT OF THE BATTLE BELOW

Yes, God chooses to substantiate His Word with manifestations. This does not imply that God works according to our impatience or demands. God's timing is not our timing; His ways are always better than our ways.

We also cannot assume that because we pray once for something, Heaven breaks through. Or if no manifestation of His work appear, it must not be His will. We know what His will is, it is written forever in the ministry of Jesus in the Gospels (and in the Acts of His disciples after that). The truth of the matter is that there can be powers and principalities trying to block answers to prayers.

Daniel dealt with this exact situation, and it took an angel breaking through the battle above him to explain what was going on. The answer to his prayer *was coming* but there was a fight going on against the ruler of wickedness in the heavenlies over Persia.

It is instructive to hear what the angel said to Daniel when he broke through:

> Then he said to me, "Do not fear, Daniel, for **from the first day that you set your heart to understand, and to humble yourself before your God, your words were heard**; and I have come because of your words. But the prince of the kingdom of Persia withstood me twenty-one days…"
>
> Daniel 10:12–13

Read that part in bold until it sinks deep inside you.

The angel informs Daniel that from the very first moment Daniel uttered his prayer, it was heard at the Throne of Heaven and the answer was dispatched. Now that sounds like our God! But, for 21 days the spiritual opposition to that answer reaching Daniel was so intense that a war ensued in the heavens above him; a war between an angel and a demonic prince, the "Prince of Persia." Daniel's persistence and Heaven's persistence were in harmony and the answer to his prayer came. That is how the breakthrough happened.[14]

This is why Hebrews tells us there is a timing element in answered prayer. There is a period of pressing in before answers to prayer arrive:

> Now faith is the substance of things hoped for, the evidence of things not seen.
>
> Heb 11:1

So how do we define faith?

Faith is the time period between our prayer first being uttered and when the answer arrives. That period of waiting is known as the "walk of faith."

Sometimes answers are delayed through spiritual warfare. This makes sense when we consider the threat to Satan's kingdom from miraculous answers to prayer. Can you imagine a world basking in answered prayer? So can he, and he hates the idea.

---

14 Compiled from *The Saints at War* by Frank Hammond, and the Audio CD teaching, *Binding the Strongman* by Frank Hammond. See the back of the book for more information.

GOD "ONE UPS" US

Other times, God hears our prayers but is really listening to our heart's desire through those prayers. These two things may not always line up; we are imperfect beings.

In such a case, our loving Father says "hold on, I envision something far greater for you than what you are praying for!" In other words, He is going to surprise you with something even better. Do you want proof of this principle? Hear it from His Word:

> Now to Him who is able to do **exceedingly abundantly above all that we ask or think**...
>
> Eph 3:20

Just when we think we know what we want and what we need, God moves us to higher ground for a greater blessing.

There is great blessing for us to know that our prayers are heard at the Throne of Jesus the moment we utter them, from a sincere and humble heart.

Now by faith we become thankful for this promise. You would be pretty excited to know your requests made it to a king on earth, right? Here we read that our prayers are reaching the throne of the King of Heaven. Being thankful that Jesus listens and hears us opens the floodgates above us, and God answers or "one ups' us in what we ask. Psalm 37 indicates:

> **Delight** yourself also in the Lord, and He shall give you the **desires of your heart.**
>
> Ps 37:4, NKJV

LIVES BUILT ON EXPECTATION

Believers are to expect supernatural acts from God in their lives. It should become an expectation in the Christian life. Experiences in the Spirit are a normal and healthy part of being a Christian. They strengthen us and our resolve to win more territory here on earth for the Kingdom. And they are God's way of providing us with a foretaste of the glory which He has in store through the resurrection of our bodies from the grave (Romans 8:23).

> Eye has not seen, nor ear heard, Nor have entered into the heart of man the things which God has prepared for those who love Him
>
> 1 Cor 2:9

ALL THINGS ARE YOURS TO DO

God told Adam and Eve to subdue the earth (Genesis 1:28). As their descendants, we have inherited their curses. But, as we become part of the 'Family of God', we inherit the blessings of Abraham (Galatians 3:29). We are co-heirs with Jesus Christ (Romans 8:17). He has been given all power in heaven and in earth (Matthew 28:18).

Authority over sickness, demons and even the elements is yours as an anointed, spirit-filled child of God. What we need to do is learn how to tap into it and exercise it.

Living in the spirit strengthens our commitment and reinforces our resolve. Spending time with and yielding to the Spirit instills greater resistance to Satan in us. Allowing the Holy Spirit to manifest His gifts through us enables us to overcome the enemy. Isaiah 10:27 says "the anointing breaks the yoke" of bondage in our lives. It is for this reason that God gave nine fruits of the Holy Spirit (Gal 5) and an equal number (nine) of the gifts of the Holy Spirit (1 Cor 12)

You can put your spiritual need on the altar of God by speaking it out in everyday language. This is asking. You can then seek your need by praying in the Spirit. Romans 8:27 says our utterances are heard by the Father, as the Holy Spirit groans or appeals for our need. From there you can knock, you can break through into the very throne room of God by moving fully into the Spirit.

The *spirit of trauma* and the unclean spirits it brings along with it hinders and obstructs the process of prayer. They scream lies in our ears and try to shake us violently from the hope we have in Jesus. They resist us having hope in answered prayer, and the hope we have in a miracle-working God. But like any other evil spirit, they are liars.

This is why it is vital that we come to know the Holy Spirit and use the gifts of supernatural abilities to respond spiritually to these attacks.

POST DELIVERANCE MINISTRY

Binding demons and driving them out demons is the first step in removing the defilement of Satan from our lives. Putting a proper hedge of protection around our mind, emotion and will is the next step.[15]

When God sent the Israelites into the Promised Land under the capable and mighty hand of Joshua, they were instructed *not to take the land all at once*. Why? Because they had to conquer an area, establish themselves, and secure it before moving on to the next area.

Our inheritance in Jesus grants us access to the Promised Land of an abundant life. Let the Lord lead the plan of attack when you are ready to conquer the land, so that like the Israelites you will take authority over an area, become established and hold on to it. Then,

---

15 Refer to *Tormented: 8 Years and Back* by Peggy Joyce Ruth for techniques on walking out deliverance. See the back of the book for more information.

be prepared to move to the next area the Lord wants to deal with.

In certain respects, deliverance is easy because it is the work of the Holy Spirit. What happens after deliverance can be the difficult part because we need to develop new thought patterns, and disciplines, to stay free and clear from further entanglements in those areas. We are instructed to "fill our house" in order to set up defenses against the enemy, who will try to convince us that we have not gained the victory over him. He is a liar.

In simple terms, what do you do in order to keep darkness out of a house? You turn on the lights and fill the house with light. It is the same in the spiritual sense where our bodies are like a house. In fact, they are called the temple of the Holy Spirit:

> Or do you not know that **your body is a temple of the Holy Spirit** within you, whom you have from God, and that you are not your own?
>
> 1 Cor 6:19

As we establish new disciplines in our life towards Jesus, our spiritual house becomes filled with light, the light of the Spirit of Heaven! No demon or its darkness will dare come near a house willed with the light of Jesus.

Everyone is unique and comes from different struggles in their past, so the Lord may have additional disciplines for you to focus on. But here is a short list of the things we can do to fill our homes with light on a daily basis. Then rest in His presence and "abide under the shelter of His wing" (Ps 91).

1. Secure the Lord as King of your life and surrender your mistakes, faults, regrets, and failures to Him

2. Allow Him to set up His throne in Your heart, and honor Him as the King who sits on that throne

3. Stay away from things from your past that would seek to draw you like a magnet into old ways of behavior or thinking. Stay away from things offered to you in the present that would quench the Spirit or disrupt the peace of God in your life.

4. Ask the Lord for the Baptism in the Holy Spirit, and then fill your house with praising Him at various points each day in your native tongue and in Heaven's tongue. Find a private, quite place to do this away from distraction (and the television, the news, and your phone). Daniel got on his knees three times a day and was admired for it by Heaven.

5. Praise Him out loud, worship Him in your heart. Speak promises from His Word over your life and those you are responsible for.

6. Read and study His Word. Fill your mind with Him and His goodness by reading about Him in Scripture.

7. Avoid becoming legalistic or set in your ways. Allow Jesus to freshen things up for you on a regular basis. He knows best.

Notice that the above list does not suggest retiring from the world, becoming a hermit or living in a cave. Recall that three of the most accomplished men in the Bible became *second in command* of entire pagan superpowers of their day: Joseph in Egypt, Daniel in Babylon and Mordecai in Persia. They were able to conduct all manners of State, be counted dependable and highly effective by their kings, while at the same time keeping their hearts and minds focused on the Lord. Study their lives.

THE ANTISEPTIC WORK OF FORGIVENESS

No problem is too great for Jesus. Most of our troubles are small in comparison to what He has already accomplished on the Cross. He will give a gift of strength to those traumatized by torment of evil spirits as you press in for your freedom.

In the day when I cried thou answeredst me, and **strengthenedst me with strength in my soul**.
Ps 138:3

One of the most powerful, antiseptic treatments that can be applied to the presence of traumatic thorns in our soul is *forgiveness*. Forgiveness has a cleansing effect (and is known to kill weeds instantly). Forgiving others goes to the roots of the weed of bitterness and resentment that we may hold against those that brought trauma into our lives. Sometimes this is a process, to learn to forgive but also keep a healthy guard around our heart.

> **Jesus understands this is not easy. He wants to carefully walk us through the process of forgiveness, not because others deserve to be forgiven but because you deserve the benefits that come from it.**

He knows that a life lived in bitterness is a life still infected by poison, and that poison keeps us sending weakness into our spirit instead of His strength to restore us and build us back up to wholeness.

9

TRAUMA CAN LEAD
TO NEW VISION

When trauma comes, evil spirits begin to circle like crows. They seek to take advantage of our moment of panic. They have willpower, and they have a goal: to make matters worse for us. They want to pull us down with them to their fate, because *misery loves company.* They have an appointed time for judgment and they know it.

> And they cried out, saying, "What business do You have with us, Son of God? Have You come here to torment us before the time?"
>
> Matt 8:29

They are such defiling creatures.

When we become aware of how they operate, the deterrent to their infiltration *is our vision.* A vision of the goodness of the Lord and His plans for us will establish and maintain stability within us in the middle of the chaos. It will guard our heart.

> For I know the plans that I have for you,' declares the Lord, 'plans for prosperity and not for disaster, to give you a future and a hope.
>
> Jer 29:11, NASB

The devil wants us to live myopically. This means to see things only in immediate view, and to not see what the Lord has off in the distance. If Satan can trap us in short-sightedness, he can bring us into despair and fear and open doors to trauma. If we have vision beyond the immediate view, we can resist and in some cases, see a larger, expanded view of the Lord and His power meant for our lives.

When we stand on the promises of God, like the one from Jeremiah above, we have confidence that God sees the end of the matter while to us it may seem like the beginning. Having promises in our heart creates a vision beyond the immediate crisis. This vision come in handy in a time of confusion and despair. But knowing Jesus, He wants to birth in us a larger vision, even if this expanded view is met with ferocity on the part of the enemy.

THE STORM ON THE LAKE

The Books of Matthew, Mark and Luke tell the story of Jesus calming the storm in the midst of a lake. When Jesus came to the front of the boat to see what was happening, he engaged whatever spiritual force was trying to wreck their mission to get to the other side of the lake.

> Then He arose and rebuked the wind, and said to the sea, "Peace, be still!" And the wind ceased and there was a great calm.
>
> Mark 4:39, NKJV

The end of the storm came when Jesus rebuked the winds and waves and commanded them to be silent. To "rebuke" something in the Greek means to speak a charge against it and admonish it.

This is not something you do to wind and waves, it is something you do the will and intention of whomever is driving the wind and waves.

What came against the disciples that day was both physical and spiritual in nature, and for a reason. The disciples had a mission, but in a greater sense that day, they had a new vision waiting for them on the other side of the lake, something that would carry them forward for future ministry.

THE CALL BY JESUS

Jesus gave His disciples a commission that day. He provided a mission, to get the boat over to the territory on the other side. With that, He went to sleep in the boat, leaving them in charge of reaching the destination.

The disciples knew where they were to go, they were seasoned fisherman and knew the area. But, they did not know why. As instructed, they went on obediently, until a traumatic encounter with Satan's fury came against them in the form of a storm.

Jesus was their Good News. Jesus was their Word of life (John 1:1). He was with them as they proceeded toward the completion of that mission. They were even in His service that day; He sent them across the lake. So in a sense, they were ministering to Him by attempting to comply with His commission.

Jesus was so confident in His Father's protection of His disciples that He went to sleep in the back of the boat.

> Love bears all things, believes all things, hopes all things, endures all things. Love never fails.
>
> 1 Cor 13:7–8

He believed in these precious followers of His, and He was acquainted with His Father's presence around them. He had sureness of hope in the outcome (hopes all things); He was prepared to endure any storm with them (endures all things). This is why He was able to fall asleep and rest peacefully. But while it may appear to us that God is sleeping, He is not. One might say that if God were to sleep, He tends to sleep with one eye open:

> He will not allow your foot to slip; **He who watches over you will not slumber.** Behold, He who watches over [you] **will neither slumber nor sleep.**
>
> Ps 121:3–4, NASB [Parenthesis Mine]

For this purpose He gives angels command over us to keep is in all our ways, especially in the midst of the storms of life:

> For he shall give his angels charge over thee, to keep thee in all thy ways.
>
> Ps 91:11, KJV

THE TRIUMPH THAT AWAITED AT THE END

There was a triumph waiting at the end of the journey, a vision-expanding encounter that would change the disciples forever. But a great storm arose, which threatened not only their lives but the very existence of the Early Church.

A mountain of rising water and waves suddenly appeared between them and their goal, their commission. It was a traumatic moment for them all, traumatic because they feared for their lives:

> "Teacher, do You not care that we are perishing?"
>
> Mark 4:38, NASB

They were going to die for sure, they thought; it was that bad of a storm. These were seasoned fishermen. They were proficient at managing the sea, rowing and steering a boat, but this storm was like few they had seen before. Why such a raging storm at this precise moment?

Satan knew that this ragtag group of men were headed into one of his strongholds. In a place called Gadara, on the opposite shore, lived a man tormented by a "legion" of demons. He had such supernatural strength that they could not keep him in chains, he would just tear them off! This had an effect on the people in that region, as you could imagine. Gadara not only had a man running naked among the graves, unchained and screaming through the night, but it had a population living in fear of the power of the evil that resided in that man.

This was an area with people governed by fear and trauma by what they saw running wild amongst the tombs.

Who was in charge in Gadara? Was it the God of peace? Was it the God of light and salvation? No, it was the god of fear, who lives in darkness and causes torment. This was the domain of the *god of trauma*. Just how bad was this man?

> When He [Jesus] got out of the boat, immediately a man from the tombs with an unclean spirit met Him. He lived among the tombs; and no one was able to bind him anymore, not even with a chain, because he had often been bound with shackles and chains, and the chains had been torn apart by him and the shackles broken in pieces; and no one was strong enough to subdue him. Constantly, night and day, he was screaming among the tombs and in the mountains, and cutting himself with stones.
>
> Mark 5:2–5, NASB

On a scale of 1 to 10, this fellow was pretty close to a 10.

Now, can you imagine the fear in Satan's eyes when he saw that boat *full of light* headed like a battering ram toward the darkness of his domain, Gadara?

Satan knew he was on a collision course with the Son of God and that the boat was Heaven's battering ram headed his way.

He knew a spiritual battle that was sure to happen if that boat arrived safely on shore.

He knew a spiritual earthquake would occur if that heavily demonized man living among the tombs showed up in his right mind, wearing clothes, calm and speaking like a sane man.

And the devil was right.

After being delivered, the man was *on fire for Jesus*. He wanted to follow Jesus wherever He went. Where there had been desperate need, this man was now dressed for battle and ready to launch in boldness for the Lord. He was full of fuel to ignite the region for Heaven's purposes. This man had caught a vision of what the Lord could do.

Jesus immediately saw this man's potential. He told this calm, worshipful man to go and tell others of the great things God had done for him (Mark 5:19). Imagine the stunned looks when this man walked into town? His mere presence, in his right mind, proved the superiority of the Kingdom of Heaven over the kingdom of darkness. And it proved it overwhelmingly.

We are told the man began the fulfillment of his ministry by sharing the wonders of God's mercy and miraculous powers. His vision began to be realized as he went from town to town, telling the good news of what had happened to him and the potential for that to happen in the lives of others (Mark 5:20). Sure enough, all men marveled at what they saw and heard (Mark 5:20).

AN EXPANDED VISION FOR THE DISCIPLES

Can we now see the powerful effect of that boat arriving on the other shore of the lake? Do you see why Satan threw a fit and sent everything he had against it, including an encounter a traumatic encounter with the fear of death?

Consider the effect this miracle had on the disciples with Jesus. They would have seen the crazy man among the tombs and probably decided it was best to leave this one alone. The place was creepy. What could they have done for that man anyway? Some are just too far gone. The disciples would have seen the situation up close, in a short-sighted manner. Without the actions of Jesus, it would have been a myopic moment for them.

But now, after Jesus stepped in among the tombs, they witnessed the power of light conquering the power of darkness in a powerful fashion. This may have been the greatest deliverance of all they saw by the hand of their Teacher, Jesus!

This experience in Gadara was *equipping*. It stole the devil's ability to convince these simple fishermen that some people are just too gross and far gone for the ministry of Jesus to have an effect. Instead,

The deliverance of the crazed man among the tombs greatly enlarged their vision to reach those oppressed by evil spirits.

They had seen with their own eyes what Heaven coming to Earth was capable of doing, and they began to envision how this ministry could happen through them. First, however, they had to make it through the storm.

YOUR STORM CAN LEAD TO EXPANDED VISION

In the case of the disciples in the boat, Jesus lay down and went to sleep. In our case, Jesus has ascended into Heaven, where He is seated Himself at the right side of the Father (Revelation 3:21).

In both cases, a vision has been established. A ministry has been launched. While we may think He is sleeping, He is there by our side and available at a moment's notice. His eyes are ever on us:

> For the eyes of the Lord run to and fro throughout the whole earth, to show Himself strong on behalf of those whose heart is loyal to Him.
>
> 2 Chron 16:9

He has put a task in our hand, just as He did with the disciples. We have something to offer the Master and we now have the authority and the power with which to do it. For many reading this, that thought may have been impossible.

Seeing what happened on the other side of the lake, and the reason so much trauma was sent against that miracle happening, we may look with new eyes on why the enemy tries so hard to wrap us in chains of trauma. And, we and we have a vision for how God can rebuke the trauma of the storm.

> **You will not die but** *live* **and** *see* **and** *declare* **the works of the Lord.**

Jesus has given all of us the same commission. He wants us to move forward with a vision.

- He wants you to be a witness for Him (Acts 1:4).

- He wants you to receive the baptism in His Holy Spirit and to speak in new tongues. This is an edifying, warfare language for us to rebuke the enemy, and to silence all his winds and waves (John 3:11, Mark 16, Acts 2, 1 Cor 12).

- He wants you to cast out demons and heal the sick (Mark 16, John 14:12

- He wants you to exercise authority over all the powers of the enemy (Luke 10:19).

- Having done all to stand, He wants to encourage you to yet stand (Eph 6:13) until He appears in His full might and glory.

May this be your vision!

TESTIMONY:
TRAUMA ATTACKS OUR MINISTRY AND OUR VISION

Eve and I had just experienced a successful weekend of ministry, and seen the Lord's mighty arm set many people free. As we left for our next assignment from the Lord, Satan tried to take advantage of our tired hearts and minds and inflict trauma on us. After about an hour on the open road we heard a loud noise from behind. As part of our traveling ministry, we were pulling a thirty-foot trailer and a noise of that nature meant alarm.

I stopped and went behind the truck to look at the spot where the trailer connects. The heavy steel clamp that holds the leveling bars had snapped; it had broken off and the bar was lying in the street.

I used some wire on hand to tie the bar back on so we could creep along slowly for a few blocks as we had learned there was a mobile home repair shop close by. By then, it was early morning, it was cold and it had just began to mist.

The man behind the counter came outside with a replacement clamp. He looked things over, and told us that his clamp was different from mine and it would not work. He said, "See, my clamp is different from your broken clamp," as he held his new clamp next to our broken one. He was the expert so we listened as he told us about a trailer hitch store that could fix it. All we had to do was cross the bridge over the river into Memphis.

We began to slowly make our way again, but by now it had begun to rain hard. It was Monday morning, with rush hour traffic building up fast, on all sides around us, and the mist had turned into a hard mid-western rain. But wait; it gets worse before it gets better.

As we headed for the shop across the river, my windshield wiper blade on the driver's side popped off and sat useless on the hood. I looked on in disbelief.

We were now in the center lane of traffic, with two lanes between us and the curb, unable to see clearly and without a way to pull over. This was rapidly becoming a traumatic moment for us, with a reason to panic.

The Lord prompted me to be still and listen. It was then that He made me realize that we were under attack. Like the disciples in the boat, we were in the midst of a traumatic storm.

I immediately spoke loudly and commanded Satan to take his hands off God's property and flee!

In some way that can only be attributed to the grace and glory of God, I managed to change lanes and pull into a service station. I picked up the windshield wiper blade from atop the hood (where it had miraculously remained), popped it back into place, and checked our bearings. I began to notice then, that after having rebuked Satan, the rain began to lighten quickly. By the time we reached the trailer hitch shop the rain had ceased!

When we met the man at the second shop, he came out with the correct clamp in his hand. But he took one look at ours and said, "Mister, your clamp is not broken, there's nothing wrong with it!"

I stared down in utter amazement as that rusty old clamp had been restored to its original condition! How is that even possible? Only the God of Heaven could have done that!

Before I could even begin to praise the Lord, the owner of the shop had something important to tell me. "What you need is to replace those leveling bars. The load you're pulling is too heavy for the size you have. If you don't change them, you could have a bad accident."

Now I could really start to praise the Lord. God turned all the devil meant for harm around, spared our lives in the midst of a storm, miraculously repaired a clamp, and put us back on the road in a safer, more blessed setup.

Not only had God kept us under his wing (Psalm 91), resolved our troubles (the rusted broken clamp), but left us better off than when the storm began (with a safe new set of leveling bars).

Satan did everything he could to get us to panic in that time of trauma, but we pressed through. We took authority and overcame the crisis by the Lord's great hand working on our behalf. Jesus is the strong, right arm of the Lord:

> For He [God] has done marvelous things; His right hand and His
> holy arm [Jesus] have gained Him the victory.
>
> Ps 98:1, NKJV [Parenthesis mine]

God prompted us to remain calm and allow Him to show us the way through the storm to bring us safely through the crisis.

The trailer was our boat. We were in a storm. My wiper blade had come off in rush hour traffic, in heavy rain, and Jesus was asleep in the back of the boat. Actually, He was in Heaven on His throne, keeping His watchful eye on us the whole time. It just felt like He was asleep in the back of the boat for a moment, until we remembered Satan is a liar!

10

WHEN HEAVEN COMES TO EARTH

When Heaven comes to Earth, trauma flees. Are we prepared for Heaven to invade our lives? Are we ready to let go and let Heaven's army invade the painful memories of our past, to break the chains wrapped around our soul, and take charge of the circumstances in our life? I know I am!

How can we know with such certainty the will of Heaven with regard to the trauma in our lives? Allow me a moment to walk you through a few powerful truths concerning the will of the Lord with regard to stress, trauma and post traumatic stress.

THE LORD'S PRAYER

One day the disciples asked Jesus how to pray. What they were really asking was, "Lord, what kind of prayers please Your Father in Heaven?" The answer Jesus gave is known as the "Lord's Prayer."

This short, simple prayer is so powerful that it provides a window into Heaven to reveal the heart of God and His will for His people. Let's take a moment to read it see what powerful truths emerge from it.

> Now it came to pass, as He was praying in a certain place, when He ceased, that one of His disciples said to Him, "Lord, teach us to pray... So He said to them, "When you pray, say:
>
> Our Father in heaven, hallowed be Your name.
>
> Your kingdom come. Your will be done on earth as it is in heaven.
>
> Give us day by day our daily bread.
>
> And forgive us our sins, for we also forgive everyone who is indebted to us.
>
> And do not lead us into temptation, but deliver us from the evil one."
>
> Luke 11:1–4

The will of God in Heaven is laid bare here in this prayer. If we had to summarize the purpose of this prayer, it would be "Heaven intends to come down to Earth."

Jesus very much wants to take the peace, the joy and the righteousness that He sees on a daily basis from His throne in Heaven and bring it to us on Earth. We see this powerful truth in the beautiful first part of the prayer. Jesus is in essence saying:

> "Father, bring your Kingdom (in Heaven) down to Earth. For when Your Kingdom comes, Father, Your will in Heaven is going to come with it. This way, Your will be done on Earth as it is already done in Heaven."

Why is this so powerful?

- Because in Heaven, there is no trauma.
- Because in Heaven, there is no post traumatic stress.
- Because in Heaven, there is no trauma-based mind control.
- Because in Heaven, there is no sickness of body, mind or emotions.
- Because in Heaven, there is no abuse, sexual or otherwise.
- Because in Heaven, there are no accidents, nothing can cause harm.

The fact that Jesus encourages us to pray for this to happen shows what the will and the heart of God is. His will is for the defilement of Satan to be removed from the face of this planet, and for people to finally experience what the presence of the true God is like. His will is to shut the mouths of the lions of trauma.

Satan is going to be purged, and those unrepentant ones who cause trauma, like him, will be purged as well. Nothing will remain that can cause defilement.

THE WILL OF GOD COMING TO EARTH

Dear child of God, this time is coming. There are many promises and prophecies that this *day is coming*, and we are fast approaching its *dawn*.

What will the world look like when the Prince of Peace comes down from Heaven to reign over the nations? Let me give you a few glimpses of how glorious this day will be:

1. Isaiah informs us that wars on Earth will cease.

    > They shall beat their swords into plowshares, and their spears into pruning hooks: nation shall not lift up sword against nation, neither shall they learn war any more.
    >
    > Is 2:4

    Can we imagine a world without the *trauma of war* and *bloodshed?* Where armies will not even train for war anymore? Where soldiers do not have to face post traumatic stress? Such will be the law of the land when the Prince of Peace is seated on His earthly throne over the nations.

2. The will of God regarding the *trauma of His people* is on display in the souls that stand around His throne in Heaven, as we wait for this glorious day to dawn on Earth:

    > For the Lamb which is in the midst of the throne shall feed them, and shall lead them unto living fountains of waters: and **God shall wipe away all tears from their eyes**.
    >
    > Rev 7:17, KJV

    God's will for His traumatized people is to feed them, to quench their thirst, and to wipe all tears from their eyes. Right now, heaven is that place.

    Try to imagine a place where there is no trauma, and no tears to be shed from past trauma, no apprehension of trauma to come. That is the place God is preparing for His people through the work of His Son on the cross.

3. So great will the impact of Heaven coming to Earth that even the animals will live in peace. Trauma will be absent in the animal kingdom when Jesus returns as the Prince of Peace. The animals will not harm each other and they will not harm man either.

> "The wolf also shall dwell with the lamb, the leopard shall lie down with the young goat, the calf and the young lion and the fatling [calf] together; and a little child shall lead them.
>
> The cow and the bear shall graze; their young ones shall lie down together; and the lion shall eat straw like the ox.
>
> The nursing child shall play by the cobra's hole, and the weaned child shall put his hand in the viper's den.
>
> They shall not hurt nor destroy in all My holy mountain, for the earth shall be full of the knowledge of the Lord as the waters cover the sea.
>
> Is 11:6–9, NKJV

Many of us have grown up on a diet of nature documentaries where we see the predatory nature of animals against one another. That all stops the moment Jesus sets foot on Earth.

The wolf will not harm the lamb, he will become harmless like a lamb in its nature. Likewise, the leopard will not chase down a goat to devour its flesh, and a lion will not devour the flesh of the calf. These animals that live off meat will instead eat grass and vegetation, as it was meant at the beginning (in Eden).

Even the serpent will lose its ability to harm, and child will be able to play near the Cobra's or viper's den without fear of being bitten.

How will all this be possible? Because the Prince of Heaven will come back to Earth and bring His Father's will with Him. The will of Satan will be purged from Earth.

When the Prince of Peace arrives, trauma will flee the nations forever.

Isaiah says the whole world will be filled with the knowledge of the Lord the way the waters cover the sea.

What is the knowledge of the Lord?

It is the knowledge of *His will for us* and *for His creation*. The whole world will be filled with the knowledge of the will of God. One demonstration of this is the absence of trauma in the animal kingdom. Another will be the absence of war.

Jesus, the Prince of Peace, will be seated on His Throne as the direct representative of Heaven itself. It is for this reason we see Jesus referred to by the prophet Isaiah as a Mighty Counselor and the Prince of Peace. While he came the first time as the "Child born to us," when He comes a second time as King, "of the increase of His peace there will be no end."

> For a Child will be born to us, a Son will be given to us; and the government will rest on His shoulders; and His name will be called **Wonderful Counselor**, Mighty God, Eternal Father, **Prince of Peace**.
>
> There will be **no end to the increase of His government or of peace** on the throne of David and over his kingdom, to establish it and to uphold it with justice and righteousness from then on and forevermore.
>
> Is 9:6–7, NASB

Isaiah says there will be no end to the *increase* of His peace when He sits on David's throne, here on Earth.

That means His peace will just keep expanding and expanding across Earth and it will never stop increasing!

THE LORD'S PRAYER FOR US TODAY

God does not change. His will in Heaven when Jesus returns is the same as His will today, which is the same when Jesus came and ministered two thousand years ago:

> Every good gift and every perfect gift is from above, and cometh down from the Father of lights, **with whom is no variableness, neither shadow of turning**.
>
> James 1:17, KJV

In other words, *God does not change.* There is no variation in God, nor does He ever turn His back on us. Even today, He is the giver of every good and perfect gift that comes down to us from Heaven.

There is so much more that could be said about the Lord's Prayer. While it is powerfully prophetic, the Prayer is meant to have a reality in our life today.

> **Jesus died that Heaven might, in some way, come to Earth in our lives now.**

The Lord's Prayer is meant to counter the effects of the god of trauma in our lives today.

The purpose of this book is to spread the good news that we do not have to wait for Jesus to be physically on Earth for the effects of trauma to flee. He sent His Holy Spirit, the Spirit of Heaven's power, to work on our behalf while we wait for His return.

> Now the Lord is the Spirit, and **where the Spirit of the Lord is, there is freedom**.
>
> 2 Cor 3:17

Yes, Jesus is coming back to set up a throne over all the nations and to rule as Prince of Peace and King of Kings. But today, He is focused on you and I, in order to set up His throne in our hearts now. He wants to reign as the Prince of Peace over weary souls, burned out nervous systems, panic attacks, and traumatized minds. This is the manifestation of the Lord's Prayer for our lives today. This is the manifestation of Heaven coming to Earth today.

This is why, not by coincidence, the Lord's Prayer ends with the promise of deliverance:

"but deliver us from the evil one."

Deliverance from the evil one includes deliverance from the evil spirits sent to cause trauma and torment. That is the Lord's Prayer for us today, in the here and now.

APPENDIX:

A PRAYER TO BREAK CURSES

LORD JESUS, I BELIEVE WITH ALL MY HEART THAT YOU ARE THE SON OF GOD. YOU LEFT YOUR THRONE OF GLORY IN HEAVEN AND BECAME A MAN. YOU LIVED IN THIS WORLD AND WERE TEMPTED IN ALL THINGS, LIKE US, YET WITHOUT SIN. THEN, YOU WENT TO THE CROSS AND LAID DOWN YOUR LIFE. YOUR PRECIOUS BLOOD WAS POURED OUT FOR MY CLEANSING AND MY REDEMPTION. YOU ROSE FROM THE DEAD VICTORIOUS OVER THE CURSE OF DEATH AND ASCENDED INTO HEAVEN. YOU ARE COMING AGAIN IN ALL YOUR GLORY.

YES, LORD, I BELONG TO YOU. I AM YOUR CHILD AND HEIR TO ALL YOUR PROMISES. YOU ARE MY SAVIOR, MY LORD AND MY DELIVERER.

I COME TO YOU IN AN ATTITUDE OF REPENTANCE. I ASK YOU TO FORGIVE ME OF EACH SIN THAT I HAVE COMMITTED — THE ONES I AM AWARE OF AND THOSE WHICH I HAVE NOT RECOGNIZED. I AM SORRY FOR THEM ALL.

I CONFESS ALSO THE SINS OF MY FOREFATHERS. I RENOUNCE, BREAK AND LOOSE MYSELF AND MY FAMILY FROM ALL HEREDITARY CURSES, AND FROM ALL DEMONIC BONDAGES PLACED UPON US AS THE RESULT OF SINS AND INIQUITIES THROUGH MY PARENTS OR ANY OF MY ANCESTORS.

I CONFESS AS SIN, AND ASK YOUR FORGIVENESS, FOR EVERY INVOLVEMENT WITH THE OCCULT, CULTS, AND FALSE RELIGIONS (BE AS SPECIFIC AS POSSIBLE). I CONFESS HAVING SOUGHT FROM SATAN'S KINGDOM THE KNOWLEDGE, GUIDANCE, POWER AND HEALING THAT SHOULD COME ONLY FROM YOU. I HEREBY RENOUNCE SATAN AND ALL OF HIS WORKS. I LOOSE MYSELF FROM HIM, AND I TAKE BACK ALL THE GROUND THAT I EVER YIELDED TO HIM. I CHOOSE THE BLESSING AND REFUSE THE CURSE. I CHOOSE LIFE AND NOT DEATH.

WARFARE PRAYER:

SATAN, YOU HAVE NO RIGHT TO MY LIFE AND NO POWER OVER ME. I BELONG TO GOD, AND WILL SERVE HIM AND HIM ONLY. BY THE AUTHORITY OF MY LORD JESUS CHRIST, I BREAK THE POWER OF EVERY EVIL CURSE THAT HAS COME UPON ME. I COMMAND EVERY DEMON EMPOWERING THAT CURSE TO LEAVE ME NOW. I BREAK TIES WITH ANCESTRAL SPIRITS, WITCHCRAFT SPIRITS AND CURSES SPOKEN OVER ME. [BE SPECIFIC IN IDENTIFYING CURSES YOU FEEL ARE WORKING AGAINST YOUR PARTICULAR FAMILY.]

JESUS IS LORD.

HE IS IN AUTHORITY OVER ME NOW!

AMEN[16]

16 Adapted from *The Breaking of Curses* by Frank Hammond

APPENDIX:

DELIVERANCE FROM THE SPIRIT OF TRAUMA

LET'S INVITE THE LORD TO MINISTER. DECLARE YOUR READINESS TO RECEIVE ALL THAT GOD HAS FOR YOU, HERE AND NOW. SAY OUT LOUD, "I AM LIVING FOR JESUS, FOR HIS GLORY. I AM LIVING FOR HIS PURPOSES AND HIS PLANS."

JESUS, I ASK YOU TO FLOOD THIS ROOM WITH THE SWEET AROMA OF HEAVEN, THROUGH THE HOLY SPIRIT. I SERVE NOTICE THAT NO OTHER SPIRIT IS ALLOWED TO DWELL IN THE PRESENCE OF THE MOST HIGH.

HOLY SPIRIT, THANK YOU THAT THIS PRAYER IS REACHING THE THRONE IN HEAVEN RIGHT NOW. WE SENSE YOUR PRESENCE, AND WE ARE GRATEFUL BECAUSE WE CANNOT DO ANYTHING APART FROM YOU.

HEAVENLY FATHER, YOU HAVE PROVIDED COUNSEL TO US – YOUR SON IS THE **WONDERFUL COUNSELOR**, THE GREAT TEACHER. YOUR SON HAS INSTRUCTED US HERE TODAY.

AND ENEMY, YOU HAVE BEEN LISTENING, TOO. YOU HAVEN'T LIKED ANY OF IT, BECAUSE IT IS POWER AGAINST YOU. IT BRINGS LIGHT AND TRUTH. YOU HATE LIGHT AND TRUTH, BECAUSE YOU CANNOT OPERATE IN THE PRESENCE OF LIGHT AND TRUTH.

YOU ARE MY ENEMY. YOU HAVE DECEIVED ME IN TIMES PAST, YOU'VE LED ME DOWN THE PATHS OF TRAUMA AND FEAR, LUST AND SIN. YOU THOUGHT YOU HAD ME ON THE ROAD TO COMPLETE RUIN. I WANT YOU TO KNOW, IT IS ALL TURNED AROUND AND IN REVERSE, RIGHT NOW BECAUSE THE PRESENCE AND THE POWER OF JESUS IS HERE.

BY A DECISION OF MY WILL, I FALL OUT OF AGREEMENT WITH ALL LIES FROM UNCLEAN SPIRITS. I AM GOD'S CHILD. I HAVE BEEN REDEEMED BY THE PRECIOUS BLOOD OF GOD'S OWN SON. I HAVE BEEN PURCHASED, BOUGHT BACK FROM SLAVERY TO SIN, AND BOUGHT BACK FROM SLAVERY TO FEAR AND TORMENT UNDER THE LORD JESUS CHRIST.

I [SPEAK YOUR NAME] HAVE BEEN WASHED, BY GOD'S OWN BLOOD. THOUGH MY SINS WERE RED LIKE CRIMSON, THEY ARE NOW **AS WHITE AS SNOW**. THROUGH MY FORGIVENESS AT THE CROSS, MY SINS HAVE BEEN REMOVED AS FAR AS THE EAST IS FROM THE WEST.

I AM FINISHED WITH THE DEVIL'S FRUSTRATIONS, AND EVERYTHING HE HAS DONE TO BIND ME UP, TO KEEP ME FROM WALKING IN FREEDOM. I INVITE THE ARMY OF HEAVEN TO DRIVE EVERY FOUL, UNCLEAN SPIRIT AWAY FROM MY SOUL, AND TO PURSUE THEM RELENTLESSLY. THERE IS A MIGHTY ARMY OF HEAVEN MOVING ON MY BEHALF, AND YOU SPIRITS ARE HEADED TO YOUR DESTRUCTION.

I SPEAK TO THE *SPIRIT OF TRAUMA* AND *FEAR*. I REBUKE YOU; I RESIST YOU. I AM **NOT** GOING TO LIVE UNDER YOUR POWER OR CONTROL ANY LONGER. FAR GREATER IS JESUS WHO IS IN ME, AND HE WILL NEVER LEAVE OR FORSAKE ME.

GOD HAS A UNIQUE PLAN FOR ME [YOUR NAME]. HE HAS A FUTURE FOR ME AND IT IS FOR LIFE NOT DEATH, FOR PEACE AND NOT CALAMITY OR TRAUMA. JESUS, I ASK YOU TO RESTORE MY HOPE.

TODAY, THE PRISON DOORS WITHIN ME ARE SWINGING WIDE OPEN. THE LIGHT OF GOD IS RUSHING IN, AND THE **TORMENT**, **FEAR** AND **TRAUMA** OF THE ENEMY ARE FLEEING.

I, WHO WAS BOUND AND OPPRESSED FROM WITHIN MYSELF, AM WALKING OUT OF THAT PRISON CELL IN JOY AND WITH PRAISE. THANKSGIVING IS IN MY HEART.

I, [YOUR NAME], WILL NOT SETTLE FOR ANYTHING LESS THAN MY FULL INHERITANCE IN CHRIST JESUS.

I, [YOUR NAME], COMMAND THE THIEF, THE LIAR, THE MURDERER, TO FLEE BEFORE THE PRESENCE OF THE LORD, AND BEFORE HEAVEN'S ARMY SUPPORTING ME RIGHT NOW.

I AM EXCITED, BECAUSE I AM GOING ON WITH THE LORD, AND LEAVING THE POISON AND THE INFECTION OF MY SOUL BEHIND. I AM GOING TO FILL MY LIFE WITH LIVING WATER, HIS WORD, AND

THERE WILL BE **PURITY** IN MY LIFE. THERE WILL BE **HOLINESS** IN MY LIFE. **GOOD FRUIT WILL COME OUT OF ME**; SO MUCH THAT IT IS GOING TO OVERFLOW INTO THE LIVES OF OTHERS AROUND ME.

I WORSHIP YOU NOW, JESUS

I THANK YOU FOR THIS MIGHTY DELIVERANCE.

I REST IN YOUR LOVE.

AMEN![17]

---

17 Adapted from the booklet *Soul Ties* by Frank Hammond

OTHER DELIVERANCE TITLES

PIGS IN THE PARLOR　　9780892280278

A handbook for deliverance from demons and spiritual oppression, patterned after the ministry of Jesus Christ. The Hammonds also present a categorized list of 53 Demonic Groupings, including various behavior patterns and addictions. Testimonies of deliverance are presented throughout the book including Pride, Witchcraft, Nervousness, Stubborness, Defiance, Mental Illness and more.

STUDY GUIDE: *Pigs in the Parlor*　9780892281992

Designed as a study tool for either individuals or groups, this guide will enable you to diagnose your personal deliverance needs, walk you through the process of becoming free, and equip you to set others free from demonic torment. Includes questions and answers on a chapter-by-chapter basis as well as new information to further your knowledge of deliverance.

CONFRONTING FAMILIAR SPIRITS
Counterfeits to the Holy Spirit　　9780892280179

A person can form a close relationship with an evil spirit, willfully or through ignorance, for the purposes of knowledge or gain. When a person forms a relationship with an evil spirit, he then "has a familiar spirit." Familiar spirits operate as counterfeits to the gifts of the Holy Spirit.

Also Available as an Audio CD
9780892283989　CD

TRIUMPHING OVER FAMILIAR SPIRITS

OBSTACLES TO DELIVERANCE:
Why Deliverance Sometimes Fails　　9780892282036

Why does deliverance sometimes fail? This is, in essence, the same question raised by Jesus' first disciples, when they were unable to cast out a spirit of epilepsy. Jesus gave a multi-part answer which leads us to take into account the strength of the spirit confronted and the strategy of warfare employed.

Also Available as an Audio CD
9780892283606 CD

Obstacles to Deliverance

FRANK HAMMOND

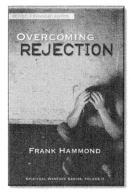

9780892284290

Overcoming Rejection

REJECTION is one of the most common, inner wounds. It can occur at any stage in life, from the time of conception through adulthood. Rejection is one of the most neglected wounds within a person's soul. It brings a disturbance and a heaviness on a human heart.

The Spirit of the Lord restores our soul, and our confidence in who we truly are. In this moment, your Savior wants to become stable in His love, and to find a new freedom from the chains of the enemy.

Audio CD: Rejection – Cause & Solution

In this practical teaching, Frank Hammond highlights the common causes of rejection in our lives, and explains how it can begin as early as in the womb. Frank explains his own battles with rejection which began early in childhood and affected his adult years as a young pastor.

9780892283941 CD

9780892280766

Forgiving Others:
THE KEY TO HEALING & DELIVERANCE

Unforgiveness is an obstacle to our walk with Jesus, and can be a roadblock to the deliverance and freedom of our bodies and souls. Frank Hammond explains the spiritual truths regarding the necessity of forgiveness and the blessings of freedom which result.

9780892280773

Comfort for the Wounded Spirit

A message of hope and healing for those who are downtrodden, bruised, crushed and broken by calamity. The Hammonds show how deliverance from unclean spirits and the healing of inner wounds are separate, yet companion, ministries. Discover How one's spirit is wounded; Symptoms of the wounded spirit; Five biblical examples of the wounded spirit; Comfort as the way of healing; Where comfort is found; How to receive healing and comfort, and more.

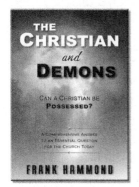

9780892284269

THE CHRISTIAN & DEMONS

*CAN A CHRISTIAN BE POSSESSED? **LIKE IN THE MOVIES?***

Can a Christian be Possessed? *Like in the movies?* This is one of the most challenging and controversial issues in the Body of Christ today. The uncertainty surrounding this issue creates an obstacle to the greater move of the Holy Spirit taking place on earth. In this concise teaching, Frank Hammond answers the most pressing questions about the deliverance ministry, and whether it applies to Christians in our time…

- HOW CAN A CHRISTIAN, WITH THE HOLY SPIRIT DWELLING IN HIM OR HER, HAVE A DEMON?
- HOW DOES DEMONIC ACTIVITY COMPARE TO WHAT I HAVE SEEN ON TV OR IN MOVIES?
- ISN'T THIS A MINISTRY FOR REALLY MESSED UP PEOPLE, BEFORE THEY ACCEPT JESUS?
- AREN'T MOST OF MY PROBLEMS PHYSICAL, NOT SPIRITUAL?
- DOES THE BIBLE ACTUALLY SAY CHRISTIANS CAN BE *POSSESSED*?

9780892283682

THE DISCERNING OF SPIRITS

Chief among the spiritual gifts in 1 Corinthians 12 - for the purposes of the ministry of deliverance - is the gift of the discerning of spirits. In this booklet and e-book, Frank Hammond explains the application of this gift to the believer, and provides examples of how it has worked in his own ministry.

Also Available as an Audio CD
9780892283620 CD

9780892283859

PRAISE: A WEAPON OF DELIVERANCE

Praise is a powerful weapon in deliverance and spiritual warfare. What happened when David began to play on his harp and sing praise to his God? The evil spirit departed from King Saul. As you praise the Lord, things begin to happen in the unseen realm. A demon cannot exist in that atmosphere — he simply cannot function.

REPERCUSSIONS FROM SEXUAL SINS
FRANK HAMMOND

The sexual revolution has impacted our nation, our church and our family. Promiscuity, nudity, pornography and sexual obscenities are now commonplace. The inevitable consequence of defilement is the loss of fellowship with a holy God. We can break free from the bondage of sexual sin!

9780892282050

THE MARRIAGE BED   FRANK HAMMOND

Can the marriage bed be defiled? Or, does anything and everything go so long as husband and wife are in agreement with their sexual activities? Drawing from God's emphasis on purity and holiness in our lives, this booklet explains how to avoid perverse sexual demonic activity in a home.

9780892281862

MINISTERING TO ABORTION'S AFTERMATH WM & SUE BANKS

The world has sold us a life without consequences. As a result, millions of women have had abortions. Those who are tormented by pain and regret of this decision have access to the throne of God to receive His mercy and love. They also have access to His mighty delivering power. Read a dozen real-life stories of women who have found deliverance and freedom from the burdens and bondage associated with abortion. Learn how their triumph can be yours!

9780892280575

DELIVERANCE FROM CHILDLESSNESS

Are you aware that the Bible has a lot to say about childlessness? Or, that demonic spirits can – in some cases – prevent childbirth? This book ministers to women and men with truths to overcome barrenness. Find the first real hope for childless couples; because for some, there is *a spiritual block preventing conception.*
BILL & SUSAN BANKS

9780892280377

A Manual for
Children's Deliverance

A book to help parents minister to children, and a valuable tool for them to learn how to set their children free from spiritual bondages. Topics include: Jesus' ministry to children, when the womb is unsafe, methods for ministering to children, occult infiltration of childhood, a child's imagination, and more.

Hammond, **9780892280780**

Deliverance for
Children & Teens

A practical handbook for ministering deliverance to children. The material in this book is arranged to help parents diagnose their children's problems and find solutions for destructive behavior. Includes a discussion of generational or hereditary issues, the role of discipline in the home, ministering to adopted children, and help for teens.

Banks, **9780892280346**

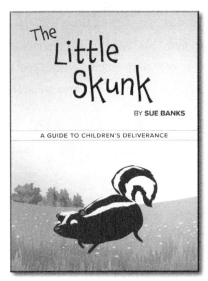

9780892281206

THE LITTLE SKUNK
A GUIDE TO CHILDREN'S DELIVERANCE

An illustrated children's story... For the child to read with a parent to understand the subject of deliverance without fear. Includes color artwork to accompany the story, and assistance at the end for the parent to pray with the child. Watch how Charlie, Billy and Susie try to get the little skunk out of their house! *Deliverance need not be frightening if properly presented.*

THE PERILS OF PASSIVITY   9780892281602

There is a purpose in God for each of us - and it is not passivity! Passivity is a foe to all believers in Christ – it can even hinder our intimacy with Jesus. Without an aggressive stance against the enemy, we can easily fall into passivity, and our service to the Lord can be limited. We lose our spiritual sharpness, which as Paul says, is necessary for us to be "sober, alert and diligent."

THE SAINTS AT WAR   9780892281046

There is a war on for your family, your city and your nation. Christians are in conflict with demons and territorial spirits. This is nothing new... the prophet Daniel confronted the "prince of Persia" when interceding for the captive people of God. Now, learn how you, too, can be involved in fighting for your family, city and nation, and in doing so, change the course of history.

SPIRITUAL WARFARE FOR LOST LOVED ONES

Through spiritual warfare, intercessory prayer, and the ministry of love, we are creating the best possible environment around a loved one to come to know Jesus. Frank Hammond says, "Don't let your family or friends go without resistance. Get in the spiritual battle, fight for your loves ones!"   9780892283842

DELIVERANCE FROM FAT & EATING DISORDERS

Help for those who have been unable to lose weight or have struggled with eating disorders. Learn about possible spiritual roots and spiritual issues related to food. This is an eye-opening look at the role food can play as a substitute for stability in the love of Jesus. Bill Banks reveals dozens of spiritual reasons for unnatural weight gain, as well as eating disorders like Bulimia and Anorexia.

Frank Hammond & Bill Banks on...
Spiritual Warfare

Praise: A Weapon of Warfare & Deliverance
We are told to resist the devil and make him flee, and praise is an often overlooked and underused weapon to accomplish this. I want you to understand what your praise does in the spirit realm. A demon cannot exist in that atmosphere — he simply cannot function. Evil spirits have tormented us enough; through praise we get to turn the tables and torment them!   Hammond, 9780892283859

9780892283842

Spiritual Warfare for Lost Loves Ones
To Bring Those You Love to Christ. Through spiritual warfare, intercessory prayer, and the ministry of love, we are able to help create the best possible environment around a loved one to come to know Jesus. But we must not lose our closeness with the Lord in the process, as these situations can be quite challenging to our spiritual walk. *"Remember that the Lord Christ is with you. The Lord is strong; the Lord is mighty; He is the Lord of hosts, the Lord of armies. He will fight in your behalf. Put up resistance and fight for your loves ones!"*

Power for Deliverance   Banks, 9780892280315
From over 30 years of counseling and ministering deliverance, in the United States and abroad, Bill Banks highlights the common root causes of emotional and mental torment, and walks the reader through steps to be set free. Includes a section on preparing for deliverance, prayers for deliverance, and keeping your deliverance.including testimonies of over 60 spirits...

Drugs	Anger	Cancer	Pornography	Perversion
Fears	Harlotry	Hatred	Witchcraft	Rebellion
Cocaine	Rejection	Temper	Occult Spirits	Childlessness
Terror	Torment	Suicide	Disobedience	Unforgiveness
Smoking	Murder	Bitterness	Homosexuality	Foolishness
Sleeping Disorder		Abuse of Women	& more!	

LEARN THE BLESSINGS OF GODLY SOUL-TIES AND HOW TO BREAK UNGODLY SOUL-TIES...

"Here at last is a thorough and theologically sound treatment of a little understood subject"
- from the Foreword by **Frank Hammond**

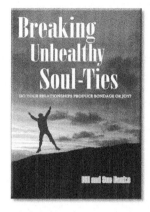

BREAKING UNHEALTHY SOUL-TIES
BILL & SUE BANKS

Unhealthy soul-ties involve the control of one individual over another, and can be a difficult block to spiritual freedom. Some relationships are healthy and bring blessings into our lives; other types of relationships can bring demonic bondage to our souls. This book assists the reader in diagnosing both healthy and unhealthy relationships, and offers positive steps to personal freedom. **9780892281398**

STUDY GUIDE:
BREAKING UNHEALTHY SOUL-TIES
BILL & SUE BANKS

This Study Guide is a tool that can be used to diagnose and address the soul-ties in your life.

This companion book provides detail into what the soul is, how it functions, and how it can be affected by both positive and negative ties. **9780892282043**

SOUL TIES   FRANK HAMMOND

Frank Hammond's booklet on Soul Ties. Good soul ties include marriage, friendship, parent to child, within christians. Bad soul ties include those formed from fornication, evil companions, perverted family ties, with the dead, and demonic ties through the church. **9780892280162**

AUDIO CD:
FREEDOM FROM DEMONIC SOUL TIES (2 CDS)

Frank Hammond teaches on healthy and unhealthy soul ties in this Audio CD, including ministry at the end for breaking demonic soul ties in our lives. **9780892283613 CD**

BREAKING OF CURSES

The Bible refers to curses over 230 times, and seventy sins that cause curses are listed in Scripture. Curses are just as real today as they were in Biblical times. Behind every curse there is a demon enacting the curse. Frank Hammond explains what curses are, and how you may deliver yourself and your family from them. Includes generational curses, cursed objects, curses spoken over people, authority–figure curses, witchcraft, and steps to breaking curses.

9780892281091

9780892284535

PHYSICAL HEALINGS THRU DELIVERANCE

When breakthroughs for physical healing occur through the casting out of spirits of infirmity... In our deliverance ministry over the years, we have seen many physical healings result from the casting out of evil spirits. We have recorded a number of these miraculous testimonies in this book (including crippling, curvature of the spine, deafness and more). This teaching identifies the most common spiritual roots of sickness, and we offer a prayer of deliverance from the enemy's harassment against our physical bodies.

Did you grow up in a home with an absent father, a missing father, or no father-figure at all?
Frank Hammond wants to introduce you to the Father's Blessing!

9780892280742

THE FATHER'S BLESSING

The body of Christ is missing out on something of great significance - *The Father's Blessing.* Through surveys in multiple conferences, Frank Hammond has found that very few persons have ever received a father's blessing through their earthly fathers. Do not despair; it's not too late! *Frank Hammond provides one for you here. You, too, can be blessed!*

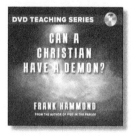

Made in the USA
Monee, IL
10 June 2023

35297313R00085